Stories of the Great Turning

edited by
Peter Reason & Melanie Newman
with a foreword by
Joanna Macy

 Vala

First published in 2013 by Vala Publishing Cooperative
Copyright © Vala Publishing Cooperative Ltd

Vala Publishing Cooperative Ltd
8 Gladstone Street, Bristol, BS3 3AY, UK
For further information on Vala publications, see:
www.valapublishers.coop or write to info@valapublishers.coop

Design and typography by Chris Seeley
Typeset in Freya, designed by Saku Heinänen
Printed and bound by CPI Antony Rowe, Chippenham, UK.
The paper used is FSC certified.

A CIP catalogue record for this title is available from the British Library.
ISBN 978-1-908363-06-0

Contents

Playing Our Part in the Great Turning
Joanna Macy

When you know where to look, you begin to see an unprecedented phenomenon taking place in this world of ours. Be they teachers in favelas, forest defenders, urban farmers, Occupiers of Wall Street, designers of windmills, military resistors (the list goes on...), people from all walks of life are coming alive and coming together, impelled to create a just and sustainable society.

In his book *Blessed Unrest*[1] Paul Hawken presents this as the largest social movement of human history. Estimating the number of grassroots groups and nongovernmental organisations for social justice, indigenous rights, and environmental sanity, he arrived at a figure of two million and counting in 2007.

Each of these groups and organisations represents a yet vaster number of individuals who, in some way or another, each uniquely in their own fashion, are hearing the call to widen the notions of their self-interest, and act for the sake of life on Earth. In this defining moment, countless choices are being made, habits relinquished, friendships forged, and gateways opened to previously unforeseen collaborations and capacities.

These actions shape stories that deserve to be told – stories of ordinary men, women and youngsters who are making changes in their minds, their lives and their communities, in order to lay the groundwork for a just and sustainable world. These are the tales that we need to hear, and those who come after us will want them as well. For, when future generations look back at this historical moment, they will see, more clearly than we can, how revolutionary it is. They may well call it the time of the Great Turning.

For us living now it is easy to be unaware of the immensity of this transition – from an entrenched, militarised industrial growth society to a life-sustaining civilization. Mainstream education and mainstream media do not provide tools for comprehending such a perspective. Yet social thinkers, such as Lester Brown and Donella Meadows and others, recognise this transition as the third major watershed in humanity's journey, comparable in magnitude and scope to the agricultural and industrial revolutions. This is the essential adventure of our time.

Like all true revolutions, it belongs to the people. Its stories do not star titans of industry or party politicians, military generals or media celebrities. The power of this revolution arises from people of all ages and backgrounds as they engage in actions on behalf of life. Their motivation represents a remarkable expansion of allegiance beyond personal or group advantage. This wider sense of identity is a moral capacity often associated with heroes and saints; but now it manifests itself everywhere on a practical and workaday plane. From children restoring streams for salmon spawning to inner-city neighbours planting community gardens, from forest defenders perched high in trees marked for illegal logging to countless climate actions to limit greenhouse gas emissions, an undreamt-of wave of human endeavour is underway.

Each of these engagements has intrinsic rewards, whether its initial goal is achieved or not. Even when failing to reach the desired outcome, the gains can be invaluable in terms of all that has been learned in the process–not only about the issue, but also about courage and co-creativity.

Still, it is easy to turn away from playing a part in the Great Turning. All of us are prey to the fear that it may be too late, and any effort essentially hopeless. Any strategy we can mount seems so puny in comparison with the mighty systemic forces embedded in the military industrial complex. The accelerating pace of destruction and contamination may already be taking us beyond tipping points where ecological and social systems unravel irreparably. Along with the Great Turning, the Great Unravelling is happening too, and there is no way to tell how the larger story will end.

So we learn again that hardest and most rewarding thing: how to make friends with uncertainty. How to pour your passion into a project when you can't be sure it's going to work. How to free yourself from dependence on seeing the results of your actions. These learnings are crucial, for living systems are ever unfolding in new patterns and connections. There is no point from which to foresee with clarity the possibilities to emerge under future conditions.

Instead of any blueprint of the future, we have this moment. In lieu of a sure-fire strategy to pull off the Great Turning, we can only fashion guidelines to help us keep going as best we can, with simple faith in the goodness of life. Here are five that have served a number of us over the years. Try them out, and make up some of your own.

1 Come from gratitude
We have received an inestimable gift: to be alive in this wondrous, self-organising universe with senses to perceive it, lungs that breathe it, organs that draw nourishment from it. And how amazing it is to be accorded a

human life with self-reflexive consciousness which allows us to make choices, letting us opt to take part in the healing of our world.

The very scope of the Great Turning is cause for gratitude as well, for it embraces the full gamut of human experience. Its three main dimensions include:

i   **actions to slow down the destruction wrought by our political economy and its wars against humanity and nature;**

ii   **new structures and ways of doing things, from holding land to growing food to generating energy; and**

iii   **a shift in consciousness to new ways of knowing, a new paradigm of our relation to each other and to the sacred living body of Earth.**

These dimensions are equally essential and mutually reinforcing. There are thousands of ways to take part in the Great Turning.

2 Don't be afraid of the dark

This is a dark time filled with suffering, as old systems and certainties come apart. Like living cells in a larger body, we feel the trauma of our world. It is natural and even healthy that we do, for it shows we are still vitally linked in the web of life. So don't be afraid of the grief you may feel, nor of the anger or fear; these responses arise, not from some private pathology, but from the depths of our mutual belonging. Bow to your pain for the world when it makes itself felt, and honour it as testimony to our interconnectedness.

When Zen poet Thich Nhat Hanh was asked, "What do we most need to do to save our world?" his questioners expected him to identify the best strategies to pursue for social and environmental causes. But Thich Nhat Hanh answered, "What we most need to do is to hear within us the sounds of the Earth crying." When we learn to hear that, we discover that our pain for the world and our love for the world are one. And we are made stronger.

3 Dare to vision

We will never bring forth what we haven't dared to dream or learned to imagine. For those of us dwelling in high-tech consumer society, replete with ever proliferating electronic distractions, the imagination is the most underdeveloped, even atrophied, of our mental capacities. And never has its juicy, enlivening power been more desperately needed than now.

So, think of how many aspects of our current reality started out as someone's dream. There was a time when much of America was a British colony, when women didn't have the vote and when the slave trade was seen as essential to the economy. To change something we need to hold the possibility that it could be different. Author and coach Stephen Covey reminds us that, "All things are created twice. There's a mental or first creation, and a physical or second creation to all things."

4   Link arms with others

Whatever it is that you're drawn to do in the Great Turning, don't even think of doing it alone. The hyper-individualism of competitive industrialised culture has isolated people from each other, breeding conformity, obedience, and an epidemic of loneliness. The good news of the Great Turning is that it is a team undertaking. It evolves out of countless spontaneous and synergistic interactions as people discover their common goal and their different gifts. Paul Hawken in *Blessed Unrest* sees this amazing emergence at the grassroots level as an immune response of the living Earth to the crises confronting us.

Many models of affinity groups and study-action have emerged in recent decades, offering methods for learning, strategising and working together. They help us uncover confidence in ourselves as well as in each other.

5   Act your age

Now is the time to clothe ourselves in our true authority. Every particle in every atom of every cell in our body goes back to the primal flaring forth of space and time. In that sense you are as old as the universe, with an age of about 14 billion years. This current body of yours has been prepared for this moment by Earth for some four billion years. You have an absolute right to step forward and act on Earth's behalf. When you are speaking up at a city council meeting, or protecting a forest from demolition, or testifying at a hearing on nuclear waste, you are doing that not out of some personal whim or virtue, but from the full authority of your 14 billion years.

The beauty of the Great Turning is that each of us takes part in distinctive ways. Given our different circumstances and with our different dispositions and capacities, our stories are unique. All have something fresh to reveal. That's why we need these stories.

Note to the Foreword
1   Hawken, P, 2007. *Blessed Unrest: How the largest movement in the world came into being and why no one saw it coming.* New York: Viking

The Story of the Book

Peter Reason & Melanie Newman

Perhaps the best way to introduce this collection of stories is to tell its own story. It's not a big, dramatic or heroic story, but like all those in the book it is about a group of people coming together to make something more than any individual could on their own. As with any story, it is the characters who made the real difference, with all their human flair and flaws, individually and together shaping an idea into something real, alive and full of possibility. And it is a story of collaboration and conviviality – linking arms, as Joanna Macy puts it – to do something worthwhile and enjoy each other's company.

When the Vala Publishing Cooperative was established, with its vision of bringing a community together to publish books "from a better world", we realised that part of this vision could be to put together a book telling the stories not of the great names and well-known figures of the sustainability movement but of ordinary people in their everyday lives. We may know about carbon emissions and climate change, about the destruction of habitats and the Sixth Extinction, about the acidification of oceans and the challenges of Peak Oil. We may read about all these issues, write to our MPs and maybe demonstrate against global apathy towards them. But what can we do in our own lives, in our homes, with our families and communities?

Sarah Bird, Vala's founding visionary and commissioning editor, was initially sceptical about publishing a multi-authored book, feeling that these too often result in a hotch-potch of contributions. "It would have to be beautifully written!" she said. And from that challenge, we developed the notion of drawing together a group of people in a temporary writing community, to help each other articulate and write their story so as to speak out as clearly as possible to a wider world.

As we developed our idea for the book, we remembered the talk that Joanna Macy had given at the University of Bath in 2005, in which she outlined five ways in which we could all participate in what she calls the Great Turning away from the Industrial Growth Society and toward a just and sustainable society. Joanna illustrated her talk with examples and poetry. Could we build upon this with individual stories that would illuminate and exemplify these five paths?

We started from the premise that telling and spreading stories of how individuals and groups are contributing to the Great Turning, of the successes and difficulties, of the ups and downs and critical turning points, is in itself a significant contribution. In these challenging times, we need stories that engage, enchant, inspire and, most of all, stories of practical changes; stories of community action; stories of changing hearts and minds. Real stories. In the words of Canon Stephen Cherry, "the creative, concrete and poetic use of words is nothing less than the spiritual effort to allow grace to speak".[1] In much of the literature on sustainability, we realised, little emphasis is placed on the poetry of words themselves, and their potential to transform.

So we sent out a call through all our networks, which was in turn passed on to many more:

Are you engaged in activities and projects, in either inner or outer spheres, that aim to contribute to building a more life-sustaining world? Would you like to share your work through creative writing? If so, we invite you to propose a chapter for this book.

You don't have to be a skilled writer, we told potential contributors, but you do have to be willing to rise to the challenge of telling your story beautifully. And those who were skilled writers, we asked to be willing to help others who were not. We invited potential contributors to join a supportive learning process that would foster creative, elegant and engaging storytelling.

We were delighted to receive more than twice as many proposals as we could include. From these we chose the ones that make up this book – and we are deeply grateful to all those who put forward ideas that we chose not to take up. Meanwhile, our initiative fired up our colleague Chris Seeley, who believes strongly that stories need to be complemented by images. She invited artists to participate in a Great Turning Artful Inquiry, a global collaboration inquiring into Joanna Macy's five guidelines through art. A selection of responses to this invitation are included in this book alongside the written stories. We have placed these artful responses as an interlude in the middle of the written responses

We invited our selected storytellers to join us in two writing workshops in Bath. The first was designed to build a supportive community to help people reflect on their experience, identify the story they most wished to tell, and explore alternative "story arcs": ways of giving structure to their account. Several months later, after everyone had written and circulated one or two drafts and received comments from us as editors and their colleagues, we held a second workshop to review and critique the near-final versions. We discussed each person's contribution in some detail with the aim of helping them tell the story more fully and more accessibly.

Both workshops were fun and productive. Many people went to great efforts to be present. Elizabeth Alberts sat at the other end of a Skype connection all day for both events. Three of the young people from Global Generation project in Kings Cross came down from London for the first workshop – their summer exams preventing them from coming to the second. Celia Sousek left her husband attending to the lambing on their Devon farm so that she could attend. We are particularly grateful to Geoff Mead, storyteller and author of Vala publication *Coming Home to Story*, who joined us for the first workshop to help us explore the nature of storytelling.

There was a warmth and vivacity in the workshops that we felt emanated not only from a shared sense of purpose but also from a sense of embarking on a journey together. We wanted the chapters to show what practical things can be done and also what personal learning had taken place as a result. We were looking for stories that were reflective and critical as well as celebratory, encouraging people to be bold and not to be afraid of dealing with setbacks, failures and experiences that might be difficult to write about. This prompted deep discussion and intense listening. It also provoked some more challenging debate about the dilemmas and differences evoked by striving to bring about change and following one's heart.

As the book evolved, it became clear that the stories did not simply illustrate Joanna's principles, but showed a far more complex pattern of challenges and responses. Practical projects are woven in with spiritual vision. Personal crises and depression lead to new inspiration. Commitments undertaken vary, disrupt or even overturn the pattern of our lives. We became particularly interested in the challenges to personal identity aroused by actively engaging with the Great Turning. There are the inner challenges – what is my place and what can I do in response to these global issues? And the outer challenges – as I become more deeply concerned and alter the way I live, how does this affect family and friends, do people see me differently, do I need to form new friendships to support my changing commitments? We explore these questions more fully in our Reflections in the final chapter of the book.

We have organised the chapters in the book so that they can be read sequentially or dipped into, one or two at a time.

There are stories which start from a practical project: Annie Davy tells of the transformation of a piece of wasteland into a community garden; Celia Sousek of moving from a suburban life to organic farming; Gil

Chambers of installing water power in a valley in Wales. Other stories start from personal crisis: Kirsti Norris explores her place in the Great Turning as a mother who is no longer able to be a Greenpeace activist; Emma Kidd discovers that her job within the capitalist world literally makes her ill and, after much searching, she creates a small business upcycling clothing into pretty underwear; tragedy in Patrick Andrews' personal life leads him to question and move away from his career as a corporate lawyer; Christine Bone is challenged by the facts of global environmental crisis to radically rethink her shopping habits; Rupesh Shah reflects on his identity both within his immigrant community and as part of the community of life on Earth.

Some stories emphasise the development of community: Jane Riddiford and her colleagues tell of initiating Global Generation, bringing together young people with industrial and commercial organisations in the Kings Cross Development; June Boyce-Tillman sets out to develop dialogue between different faith communities; Johannes Moeller creates an educational programme in which young people can find their place in a changing and confusing world; Elizabeth Alberts gets deeply involved in the onshore support for Sea Shepherd, a marine wildlife conservation organisation.

Other stories are about bringing people together in different ways to explore their concerns about the state of the world: Clare Power gives an account of a ritual gathering which offers a place to express emotional responses to the crises of our times; Helen Moore tells of a community arts project that included an exhibition of artwork and a Funeral for Extinct Species processing through the streets of her small town; Helena Kettleborough writes about how she has involved family and community in her appreciation of the scale and wonder of the universe in which we live, and her daughter Nora gives her response.

We offer this brief review of the chapters as a starting point, conscious that none of the above descriptions do justice to the richness of each story. In the closing chapter, we have attempted our own reflections on the depth, the learning and the continuing questions that we found in the stories and their compilation. It has been a profoundly moving experience, often inspiring awe and frequently the re-enforcing and revisiting of our own concerns, frustrations and aspirations, but most of all it has been one that gives us hope.

Finally, many thanks and appreciations are due. We are grateful to Joanna Macy for supporting our project and providing us with a Foreword and framework. Sarah Bird at Vala Publishing held her faith in our project and made helpful suggestions from the beginning. The contributors to the book have joined in our experiment with enthusiasm and hard work. They have taken comments and criticisms from their editors and colleagues in good part, responding willingly and creatively.

We are grateful to Geoff Mead for his contribution to the first workshop, and to Chris Seeley for the inspiration of the Artful Inquiry and for the detailed work of designing the book. The School of Management at the University of Bath provided (quite unofficially) space where we could hold our workshops and the Skype facilities that helped us include contributors from further away. Thanks to Vala Cooperative members Alan Blakemore and Denis Kennedy for the careful work of copyediting and proofreading. Many other Vala Cooperative members have been enthusiastic and curious supporters; we are honoured to be part of this wonderful experiment in community publishing.

Joanna has already referred to Paul Hawken's book *Blessed Unrest*[2], in which he describes "the largest movement in the world", the diffuse and leaderless movement that represents "humanity's willingness to restore, redress, reform, rebuild, recover, reimagine and reconsider". He writes, "If you look at the science that describes what is happening on earth today and aren't pessimistic, you don't have the correct data. If you meet people in this unnamed movement and aren't optimistic, you haven't got a heart." We are proud to be a small corner of this world-wide movement.

Notes to the Introduction

1   Cherry, S, 2012. *Healing Agony*. London: Continuum, p.113
2   Hawken, P, 2007. *Blessed Unrest: How the largest movement in the world came into being and why no one saw it coming*. New York: Viking

1
What Place is This? Story of a Garden
Annie Davy

Prelude: Year 2002

A blackbird sings beneath an azure sky. The carcass of a burned-out Ford Mondeo throws a skeletal shadow against an asbestos garage door. There are cracks and small craters where the buddleia and dandelions break through the thick concrete, but the carpet is mostly human litter. Bits of metal, the origins of which are no longer recognisable, are tangled with brambles, plastic, cans, hypodermic needles and condoms. I am standing "in my back yard": a plot of land behind my house, about the size of a football pitch, on which 24 garages are crumbling through disuse and neglect. Recently the newspapers reported the death by drugs overdose of a local man here. It feels like a place at odds with itself. Despite its sad recent history, my senses hum with life as I stand here: alone with the buzz of bees; with the smell of the briar rose; with the sight of the lilac climbing in over the tangled cross-wired fence.

A tortoiseshell butterfly passes me by. I close my eyes and reach for a palpitating sense of the life within the earth beneath the concrete, in the force of the weeds, and swirling around with the birds and the breeze of the air. There is also a deep peace here. I tremble slightly with a sense of excitement and understanding. There is a garden, waiting to be released.

A sense of place

This patch of land is a handkerchief in the easterly pocket of Oxford's city suit, just off the Cowley Road. Access for humans is via a litter-strewn corridor, a bike path alongside a ditch with frogspawn and blossom in the spring, and sloe berries and damsons in the autumn. Commuting cyclists pass dog walkers, pram pushers and pot-smoking young lurkers on their way to or from school.

This part of the City is where Gown meets Town, where transient students jostle with migrant refugees in a multi-national melting pot. There is an edge to this area, sometimes an uneasy edge. More and more family houses have been converted into houses of multiple occupation.

Care workers regularly do their rounds: visiting the elderly, the housebound and the mentally unwell. The area doesn't have a neighbourhood name – unlike Florence Park, St Clements, Temple Cowley or "The Leys". It doesn't have a library or a community centre. There are no local shops on this side of the road. It is a thoroughfare, and throughway. When I moved here with my three children it felt like an artery that was in need of a heart.

Consultations over several years led by the City Council on what should happen to the garages had not generated any change and meanwhile the fly-tipping, rubbish-burning and anti-social behaviour had increased. That day, standing in the garage site sensing the garden-in-waiting, galvanized me to take action. I had felt a call I could not ignore. After years of campaigning on global issues, here was something concrete I could do in the street where I live. But this land belonged to the City Council and the job of transformation was way beyond what I could do on my own. It would need a wider vision, motivation and capacity for action. A note through nearby letterboxes led to responses from five local residents – all interested in the idea of a community garden.

2003 – 2007: A long gestation

We watered the tiny shoot of the idea of a community garden around the kitchen table. Initially just six of us pooled our ideas and had countless conversations with our wider networks of friends and acquaintances. When we thought we were ready, we took our idea to the City Council's area committee meeting. Little did we know it was just the beginning of a protracted political game entangled in bureaucratic red tape.

My daughter Ella: *When I was twelve my mum took me to the Cowley Area committee meeting. She said I should see local democracy in action. People sat around and talked interminably about parking and rubbish. My mum told them about her idea for a garden behind our house – where the broken down garages were. They said "good idea – but go away and do a feasibility study." I asked what that was. After that there were lots of meetings in our kitchen. Once a reporter came and interviewed me about the condoms and needles by the garage site gate and the noises we heard on summer nights from our garden that backed on to the lane… I remember thinking that what I learned about local democracy was that it is very slow and very boring: too much talk, too many meetings…and still there was no garden.*

Oxford Mail 28th February 2003
Garden plan bid for death site garages

The ex-girlfriend of a man who overdosed on heroin and alcohol in a derelict east Oxford garage has welcomed moves to transform the site into a garden...

Catherine Blundell was devastated when John McGuigan, 44, was found dead at the block of garages, off Barracks Lane, in July 2000. An inquest recorded a verdict of accidental death. She said she was heartened by news the 24 city council-owned garages could be redeveloped as a community garden and education facility.

She said: "What a wonderful idea. It is a scandal that valuable land in Oxford is so neglected."

In retrospect the five frustrating years it took before we were finally granted a lease seem hazily far away. I don't want to underestimate the barriers we faced, the tears of frustration at the seemingly endless delays. Now I want to describe the series of obstacles put in our path as a dance we were required to step to until those calling the tune finally ran out of puff. And the words go something like this:

Lyrics to the Pointless Dance or, how to stifle a new idea

We like your idea but
...how will you see it through?
Get registered as a charity
...then we'll see what we can do.
We like your idea but
...we need to ask the locals
oh you are the locals?
Then admit it,
you have a biased point of view.
Oh yes, we've seen your survey
and your petition, thanks a lot
but protocol and regulations
mean consulting tenant's federations,
plus we really need to take
at least one more survey of the plot!

17

We like your idea
…but have you really thought this through?
Who will do the maintenance
and be your health and safety crew?
What about the vandals,
and the people tipping waste?
We need to talk to the police…
no need for so much haste.
We like your idea but
…we need to know still more
Prepare for us a business plan
an environmental impact report…
a risk assessment too,
You really need a lawyer,
As you do not have a clue…
We like your idea but
now we think we want to build
houses for the needy
so please don't be so greedy
as to expect to have the land
handed to you on a plate!
We like your idea but
now we are less sure.
You've greeted our resistance
with remarkable persistence
You meet all our criteria
but we do not like your hysteria
or the trouble you have caused.

Despite all the setbacks there was a still small but committed group of local people willing to develop the proposal further. Despite the stalling and frustrations, not everyone got downhearted – or at least not everyone at the same time.

Jane: *For me being part of the Barracks Garden Community Project in the early days was a joy… crowded around the kitchen table in Kenilworth Avenue, waiting for approval from the council, poring over the designs, writing grants and drinking lots of wine!*

We went to funders who said, "You might well fit our criteria – but please get formal support from the City as the landowners first." We went back to the City and they said, "We won't approve anything until you can show us you can get the funding first." We did the paperwork, became a charity, and got "incorporated". Some of the original core group became our first elected Trustees. It suddenly became a very responsible task as we were managing large contracts for land development and dealing with lawyers, leases and funding agreements. "Incorporation" meant that we had limited liability but also a range of new reporting requirements – to Companies House and to the Charity Commission. Trustees are elected each year – and a third resign each year in rotation.

We got help from so many unexpected quarters. We worked hard to drum up support, running "Swap Shops" and tea stalls in the concrete alleyway and at the local allotments open day. People started to say hello to one another in the streets around.

Helen (one of the core group and a local teacher): *Bringing my class to do a planning and a design for a community garden on the site was great fun. It was fantastic to be able to involve the children in a "real" project – one which they might see turn into reality and be able to visit as they grow up in the community. So much learning is "virtual" now. This was a real experience that led to some very imaginative ideas and models which went into the final design.*

Another spanner in the works

We were close to getting both funding and planning permission when another obstacle hurtled towards us. The environmental survey required as part of our change of use planning application showed unacceptably high levels of toxicity in the soil underneath the concrete. "You need to dig out at least six spades deep and remove the soil to a contaminated landfill site," read the report. That would mean heavy diggers, transport and skips. Our budgeted costs were suddenly tripled. Would anyone fund us to that level?

Josh (local musician and early friend of the garden): *At the beginning of 2007, my partner Sarah and I dreamt up an intimate Oxford gig with some of our favourite musicians and poets. We all decided we wanted to give the money to a worthy local cause and Sarah had heard about the Barracks Lane dream-that-was-soon-to-become-reality from a friend who was involved in the project. After finding out a bit more, and visiting the site – which was then just concrete wasteland – we were left in no doubt where we wanted to put the proceeds.*

Our compere was local poet, Stephen Hancock. I particularly remember an extract of a poem that he performed that night:

this land is an earthy barricade
this land is an earthy serenade
this land is an earthy cascade
of root, fruit, shoot, leaf, flower
of pod of sod of
fodder for stomach, heart and soul
Comrades in spades!
Let a hundred courgette flowers bloom!

let allotments roll higgledy piggledy across the land
like a harlequin's haphazard cloak of earthy hues
Comrades in spades
we have nothing to lose
but our neonic, demonic, necrophiliac, necrophobic
supermarket chains!

More Power to our Elbows!
All Power to the Allotments![1]

That fundraiser was a great success. More than the money raised, our hearts were warmed. There was strength to go on and more good news. The environment officer suggested we could go for tax relief on the landfill. The contractor was helpful and cooperative and the funders were sympathetic. That winter we could finally go ahead and the diggers move in.

2007 – 2009: Birth and early years

On 16th June 2007, at the official opening of the garden, the leader of the City Council received a ceremonial single peppercorn as the agreed annual rent. Our local MP planted a tree. We danced a mad jig in the newly erected yurt – a beautiful Mongolian-style tent and our only shelter.

At the unofficial opening ceremony a more informal group of close supporters shared a bowl of cherries and used the pips to plant their blessings and wishes for the garden. Phil sang "The World Turned Upside Down" – aka "The Diggers' Song" – and we "beat the bounds" of the garden with drums, saucepan lids and wooden spoons.

In the first years of opening it was the artists who brought creative guidance and a lot of play into the garden.

Jane (trustee): *After a year things slowly started taking shape. Those lovely days in the first months: the building of the cob oven, the yurt going up and Stig painting the shed… One of my favourite evenings was the first lantern-making workshop and afterwards cycling home with the lantern I'd made stuck on the back of my bike. It stayed lit all the way home.*

Katie (our first freelance coordinator): *I started working in the garden before it opened, organising the events programme and inviting artists, musicians, and ecologists to come and run activities. What was really exciting was the openness of everyone involved, an openness to creativity, and to how the social life of the garden emerged. I think what I saw over the first year or two was that not everything we did worked, but that slowly and steadily that openness allowed the garden to be defined by the community around it, so it really belonged to them. I feel proud to have helped it grow and to hear that it is still going strong.*

Generosity begets gratitude that opened hearts, and was in turn rewarded and nourished by the gifts and the joy of others. The years of frustration became a faded memory. The garden's infancy has drawn a circle of support around it that grew stronger as the first new plants survived the winter's frosts and continue to blossom.

2009 – 2012: Coming of age

Much as a child learns to say "I" around the age of three, the garden took three years to find its feet, to gather the community in and to start to really weave its magic. Trees were planted and then bore fruit. The birds dropped seed from the surrounding area. Roses clambered from neighbouring gardens back over the fresh new wooden fence.

Right up to the present day people who come for the first time are full of questions. What kind of place is this? Who does it belong too? What can we do here? Who decides? On high days and holidays children are often seen running barefoot through the puddles as families build sandcastles in the large sandpit made from old railways sleepers, which, if you squint, look like groynes upon a beach.

There has been "guerrilla gardening" too: oak saplings sprung from acorns pressed by children into the raised beds; the herbalists planted comfrey, lavender and rosemary; the Italian neighbour planted a fig and an olive tree to remind him of home. There have been horticultural debates over whether we should stay local and plant only native species, or whether planting needs to reflect the multi-cultural mix of the local community.

Practical projects have included rainwater harvesting and the construction of compost loos. A project with Oxford Brookes University architecture students led to the green-roofed shelter and a solar power system. The local Permaculture Group meets regularly on the site and runs courses in the yurt. Local Asian families wanted a tandoor – so now we have two ovens to cook on, as well as the fire pit.

Jackie (local musician and friend of the garden): *When my husband first talked to me about the plans for a community garden, and I peeked through a rickety gate to see a derelict patch of concrete, I have to admit I didn't get it. My powers of visualisation were not up to the job. Years later, I was playing music to an appreciative crowd of people in the lovely wooden octagonal building and the thought occurred to me, "This is like being in the summer house in a grand country estate. Except that this garden belongs to all of us!"*

In 2010 we "won" the Lottery, or rather we were successful with a three-year grant to run a Local Food Programme of workshops, demonstrations and celebrations of local food.

Looking back over the events of those first five years, they seem to read like nursery rhyme or jolly ditty:

Seedy Sundays,
Swap your plants,
Learn the art of Keeping Bees.
Herbs for Health,
Round the World Cooking,
Pressing Apples from our Trees!
Pruning, Preserving,
Making, Baking
All in ovens built of clay!

Permaculture
Forest Gardens
Dancing in the May!
Make some Compost
Keep your own Chickens
Anything else you might want to know?
About how to plant
How to pick, to prune,
and how to Make Your Garden Grow!

Lorraine: *I took my chickens to Chicken Day. The girls loved it – running around and being petted. Because of the chickens, I haven't done much in my own garden, so when I have visitors the Community Garden is a great place to take them. They are always overwhelmed. It is such a great story and talking point – and it is in my area, on my doorstep. That feels quite special.*

The garden has lent itself as a place of celebration – Mayday morning dancing, family picnics, baby-naming ceremonies and parties for children and adults.

As more visitors were attracted to the garden and it became greener, more established and known, we felt the multiplier effect from the positive feedback we received. We were successful in further grant applications and even won some local awards. We developed new partnerships with mental health, refuges and disability support organisations. We delighted about our new accessible compost loo.

Ella: *Having lived away from home for two years, coming back to see what the garden had become was amazing. The cob oven, the green-roofed shelter, the renewable technologies and the number of people having a good time was more than I could have imagined as a 12-year-old girl accompanying my mum to all those council meetings. I tease my parents that the garden became their surrogate child.*

Central to the garden has been the role of freelance co-ordinator, undertaken in different years by Katie, Alan and now Julieanne. Each brought different skills and wove new threads into the fabric of the garden with enthusiasm and love. With their support, an evolving group of volunteers – our Garden Guardians – have kept the garden open to the public every weekend from March to November ever since it opened.

Julieanne: *There is something about the space that holds a sense of happiness. It makes me feel hopeful the world can be a better place.*

And then there was more to tend than the physical garden. For the first time there were more people willing to stand than there were places to fill on the twelve-strong committee. As the garden matured we questioned our organisation and capacity to meet the expectations of visitors, volunteers and funders. We wanted to stay local and we didn't want to employ staff, but we wanted to maintain our values and integrity.

What is an ecological form for organisational and community development?

We developed these questions to help us:

1 What is it that the community want to plant next in terms of new projects?
2 How will new ideas and developments be seeded?
3 How will we ensure they fall on fertile ground and there is energy to see them through?
4 Who will tend and water and how can we be clear about roles and responsibilities?
5 How can former trustees and past events become compost for the future, sharing their experience and supporting new people to take on bigger roles?
6 What processes or habits that we have grown are in need of pruning?
7 Who are the pollinators? How can we remain open to new ideas?
8 What tools are needed now? What training, expertise or skills?
9 How can we share our harvest with others and ensure we celebrate together and continue our work with joy and gratitude?

As much as the physical garden space needed attention and development through workdays and working parties, so the social structures, systems and processes needed to be carefully nurtured and maintained. The trustees and volunteers became gardeners to the health and vitality of both.

Postscript: 2012 and beyond

I am sitting on the edge of the flowerbed listening to a group of sparrows, apparently arguing about their nesting site in the hawthorn hedge. I watch as they dive down for a communal bath in the slowly-filling pond. The quince and plum trees are in blossom and I relive the taste of the jams and jellies made in the autumn. I wonder what will grow this year.

A cloud covers the unusually warm March sun and I feel strangely both happy and sad, and a little fearful too. I remember that Chris told me that before there were garages and toxic waste, this land cradled allotments where he went scrumping as a child.

I wonder what will happen if the lease is not renewed. What if the place is vandalised? What when the current community around the garden move on or die? Who will care for it? Who will harvest the fruit? I wonder what this piece of land has seen over the 4.5 billion years of Earth's existence. I remember my keen sense ten years earlier of the garden seemingly waiting to emerge from beneath the concrete.

The cloud passes and the birds recommence their chirping – even louder than before. Five golden years have passed since the opening day, when the garden's newborn lungs started breathing. Since then, this land has inspired and nourished thousands of visitors – of all ages, from near and far, humans, animals, insects, even worms. Especially worms!

In its recent existence, the Community Garden has entered into a dance with all of those who have played and prayed, sung and sown, loitered and learned, dug and hugged on its fertile dance floor. The Garden seems to give a little shiver with delight, but perhaps it was just the breeze. Whatever comes next cannot diminish the present.

Notes to Chapter 1

1   From *All Power to the Allotments* courtesy of Stephen Hancock (*http://www.pigandink.com/*)

2
Finding My Place in the Great Turning
Kirsti Norris

I climbed the rope ladder and settled myself in a corner of the tree house. Peeping out of the window I could see my dad digging in the vegetable patch. My mum was in the house. My brothers were making a den down the end of the garden. I pulled the folded up magazine pages out of my pocket where they had been carefully concealed since ripping them out of the magazine my Gran had left behind on a recent visit. Here, in my own space, I could have a proper look at the pictures. I looked at the image of the dead elephant lying on the ground, her tusks hacked off, making her head shape quite difficult to recognise, her baby calf standing next to her. I struggled to understand the emotions stirred from seeing such a powerful, beautiful, strong creature fallen and mutilated by someone in the name of money, with no regard for her or her calf. Torn between finding it gruesome and needing to look, both sickened and fascinated. Looking back, I realise why I felt the need to hide away to look at the picture. No one would have objected to me looking at it, but I had needed my own space to allow the different emotions to run through me undisturbed.

Did the calf watch her mother being slain? How must it be feeling? How was it going to survive? These poachers, could they really not have any compassion, any feelings that the elephants are so similar to us, that they have emotions and are social beings? And if they did, what or who had led them to do this?

I spent some time looking at the pictures. As my emotions turned to questions, and my questions could not be answered, I carefully folded up the pages and pushed them deep down again into my pocket. I went back down the ladder to the garden, and carried on with my day. I had a go at trying to balance on my bike, and then became absorbed in mixing up magical sludge from soil, sand and leaves.

Throughout my childhood images of an unbalanced relationship with the natural environment continued to affect me. My parents donated money to Greenpeace, and I spent hours looking through the magazines they sent us, full of pictures of people committed to preventing destruction. I felt so pleased that people were out there, standing up against the injustices, and telling the world what was going on, getting between the whale and the harpoon, or spraying seals with paint to make their pelts worthless. I wanted to be out there with them.

The need to act grew as I grew. I became aware that not everyone shared my family's values, which I had taken to be the norm. Continually as a child I would find my bedroom light being turned off when I was reading, and turning around to see the hand on the light switch "Do you need this on?" "Uh, well, I suppose not." I was shocked one day playing round a friend's house when the mum threw the empty ketchup bottle in the bin. I was amazed! I questioned more and more why doesn't everyone take more care of the environment?

I saw my opportunity when I was sixteen. Discovering that a college in the area had a Greenpeace group determined my choice of where to study. I couldn't wait to get involved.

Within a month I was involved in my first Greenpeace action. A new Tesco store was opening in Southampton. Greenpeace were aware that this new store had failed to install CFC-free refrigerators, an opportunity sorely missed when the technology existed. Here was a chance for Greenpeace to publicly urge Tesco and other supermarkets not to ignore this issue. After much planning and preparation, and a sleepless excited night, the morning had come. Full of adrenalin, we pulled up at the new store. Already parked opposite the main entrance was an articulated lorry, emblazoned with "Tesco Fiasco". We piled out of the car and, joined by others, swiftly assembled a line of five painted coffins spelling out "T-E-S-C-O" to announce our arrival. The lorry was opened, revealing a display of the new Greenfreeze CFC-free refrigerators and freezers that could have been installed in the shop. The store manager looked between the growing queue of new customers and us. The police were called. Nervously I watched as the policeman entered the lorry and chatted to the Greenpeace people inside. He stepped back outside where I was, looked at the coffins, smiled and wished us luck. He walked over to the store manager, had a brief word, then drove off. I couldn't believe it, and from the face of the manager, nor could he. The local journalists duly turned out for opening. The front page of the local daily newspaper featured a huge photo of the lorry with us standing outside of it. The smart new stand for the Daily Echo was empty in the store that day.

This was to be the first of countless Greenpeace actions. In the following years, I would visit the oddest of places, often wearing equally odd costumes – a missile in the US spy base Menwith Hill, Homer Simpson in Sizewell B, a puffin outside McVities biscuit factory. I have sailed in the Rainbow Warrior II, conducting cetacean surveys, and spent many cold hours chained to someone or something. I was home at last. I was doing what I needed to be doing. I became involved in the Newbury Bypass campaign, joining the protest at every spare moment. In fact, my life became absorbed by campaigning – against the Criminal Justice Bill; against fox hunting; whatever the campaign, I was in, and in the various means of involvement deemed necessary! It felt right, and it felt powerful to bear witness, protest and take "holding action" to slow down, or in some instances actually stop damage to nature. I regularly used to look around me at college and get frustrated by the fact that the majority of these people were oblivious to the environmental destruction going on around them. As long as they gossiped, shopped, and went clubbing, the world would go round. Doesn't anyone else see what's going on? Don't they care? Why don't they do something?

My dear parents didn't escape my frustration. A typical teenager, I refused to acknowledge the great childhood they had given me and instead questioned how they could be satisfied just paying their Greenpeace subscription and doing the occasional door-to-door collection. Why don't they get out and actively campaign? I realise now what I didn't appreciate at the time: that everyone has different roles to play in the Great Turning. What I also didn't realise at the time was that I was still to have quite a difficult journey in finding what my role in the Great Turning might be.

One day it was my dad's turn to challenge me. "This is all too late, the road's going to be built. You need to be influencing decisions at the planning stage." I reeled off the well-versed argument "we may not win this battle, but we will win the war." The Newbury Bypass was the start of a huge road building programme in the UK and we were determined that even if we couldn't stop this part of it being built, the extra expense and delay caused by the protests would stop the rest of the programme. I said that it was impossible to know when these things were being planned; often there was little choice but to protest once decisions were made. I'd had similar conversations many times, and it was dull. It seemed that standing up for what you believe in gave everyone the right to question. People in the pub, at college, police officers, security guards. My best teenager skills shrugged off the challenge, but it kept re-playing in my thoughts. It was true, I mostly acted at the point of stopping destruction once it had already begun, and I realised it would be more effective, and less muddy, to be involved earlier in the process. I started playing with the idea of having some authoritative input into projects that might be environmentally destructive, of being respected and listened to by those with decision-making powers. I considered that even if this didn't happen, extra knowledge and expertise would help me in my campaigning.

I moved to Bristol to start a degree in environmental quality and resource management. It wasn't long before I'd found the local Greenpeace group where I continued to develop my less conventional skills in direct action, campaigning with the local group, and training others to do the same. I managed to balance time so that I could pursue both the conventional study and my activist role too. When I achieved the degree it felt like a powerful tool that I could use to be seen and heard from an authoritative position. I was keen to try out what this new lever could do!

Very quickly after graduating I got a job in an insurance company in Bristol, developing their environmental management system. This was all new to me, where people wore suits and respected a strict hierarchy. Whilst finding the situation stifling, I also quite liked the challenge, and quietly called it "working from within". I needed to gain respect as a professional, and fit in with those around me in order to be listened to, and make a difference. As I walked to the office each day, I removed my beads, necklaces and bracelets. I had dressed as an eyeball, a chicken, and even John Major whilst "working on the outside". The suit I wore to work felt like any other costume.

Giving up Greenpeace crossed my mind, but I never seriously considered it, preferring to keep my two worlds apart. I took days off work to take part in actions, and when asked what I would be doing on my day off, would give a vague response. After a while a couple of colleagues became friends and would guess what these vague responses really meant. One day my partner Steve texted me "Got the Big Issue today. Whole page photo in it of you chained to pump! Got a copy for you. Well proud of you xx." Sure enough, when I got home there it was, a full colour picture of me locked to an Esso petrol pump. Turning on the television, I saw that the same image appeared three times a day on the local news opening credits. There was no hiding it was me. Back at work, senior managers came past my desk, with eyebrows raised, commenting, "now I know where you were last week on your day off." Whilst bursting with pride for the successful action I had been a part of, I kept this hidden, instead seeing, although perhaps only imagining, their disapproval. Convinced they were wondering why they had unleashed this eco-activist into their company, questions of whether I could carry on balancing both roles became ever present. I didn't check what my managers really thought, but instead tried harder to put on a professional air, and keep my activist out of the office.

At around this time, I was called to court for another Greenpeace action I had been involved in. Days off work to attend court went under the guise of visiting friends. Getting charged didn't feel like a big deal. I knew I had done little wrong compared to those whose eco-crimes we had raised awareness of. I believe that sometimes it is necessary to break the law in order to expose and sometimes stop environmental wrongdoings. The trouble was, I was sure the company I worked for wouldn't share my beliefs, especially as they specialised in legal advice. I realised I was treading a very fine line.

Growing increasingly concerned that my two worlds could not co-exist, I needed to understand more about where I should be directing my attention. Enrolling on the Master's course in Responsibility and Business Practice at Bath University gave me the space and discipline to try to understand what I should focus on. My course mates challenged my assumption that my work colleagues would think negatively of my activism and urged me to seek feedback for myself. Upon asking a trusted confidante, I was amazed to hear her response, "you're someone with passion in what you do, you're someone that gets things done." It was really positive, and started to make me see that my strong values were actually beneficial to the company. The realisation that my activist traits of tenacity and passion could actually be helping me in my professional role, not hindering it, was a real eye-opener. It felt such a relief, and I started searching for other skills within me that I had kept in one role or another. The possibility and playfulness of allowing my different selves to dance between these areas where they had previously been self-prohibited from was liberating.

It was at this point I discovered I was pregnant. Immediately my activist work was reluctantly put on pause (climbing ladders and running from security guards seemed unwise). A couple of days before my daughter was born, I started maternity leave. My life changed instantly.

As any mother knows, being pregnant, and having a baby, is a highly emotional time. Hormones are all over the place, and being responsible for this new being was daunting. My daughter was the first baby I had really ever held, so I felt out of my depth. Maisie wouldn't feed from day one. Images of relaxing times soothing your baby quickly disappeared as the reality of this baby with no interest in feeding dawned. Determined to give her the best start in life, I resolved to keep trying, but when the stress for us both got too much, I turned to expressing milk for her. The next six months became a round of feeding and expressing day and night. I was exhausted. Promises to at least continue with the local Greenpeace group's accounts looked unlikely to be kept as the receipts started piling up in the corner of the study. I had made a vow before the birth that I would take a year off work, imagining the baby asleep in a cot whilst I did some gardening or ploughed through the reading for my Master's. The reality was so very different.

It dawned on me that from now on, Maisie would be my number one. Not activism, not work, but Maisie. I could have taken a much easier route and fed her powdered milk, but I saw this as a compromise that I refused to make. If I couldn't compromise in these first few months when my old life was so fresh in my mind, when would I? I knew I never would. I realised that activism really was on long-term hold (not just "whilst-pregnant" as I might naively have thought before). Whilst struggling to balance work with activism, I had never seriously considered stopping my Greenpeace work. This being a necessity now felt strange. I thought that it would be a real loss of identity, but actually in the chaos of emotions and normality being changed so vastly, this seemed just another adjustment. Necessary but incredibly uncomfortable. I was responsible for bringing this child into a world that was being destroyed. If there was ever a time I should be stepping up and doing more to save the planet, it was now, but here I was taking a breather.

Joanna Macy had given a lecture at the University of Bath the year before. She talked of not feeling like you are "abandoning ship" when you step back from the "holding actions of slowing down the destruction", but to see it more in terms "of stepping back…to do something else in the Great Turning…just like geese flying in formation", taking turns at the front, then slipping back in formation to rest. While she spoke, I drew the image of birds in formation in my notebook. As I stepped back from activism, I thought of this drawing. I took reassurance from Joanna's words, and realised that I needed to take my turn to make those positive influences in my daughter's life as my parents did for me. Here was a change-maker of the future who needed me.

My questioning had now shifted away from work and activism, to understanding how I would combine motherhood with whatever my role in the Great Turning might be. This seemed quite a challenge. With the arrival of the baby and all the additional bits and pieces she needed, I was very conscious of how this extra person was significantly increasing our household environmental impact that Steve and I had worked so hard to reduce. I needed to tackle this, but more pressingly, the deadline was looming to find a topic to focus my studies on for my thesis. Then it struck me that the answer to both problems was staring me straight in the face, and perhaps more frequently than I wished.

Nappies – and lots of them! I intended to use cloth nappies in place of disposables, but just could not seem to get started with this. I started noticing my inner voices. Those ones that niggle and give any excuse under the sun to not do something that you know you should be doing. Just this once, I wondered, couldn't we "forget" about the environment and carry on with convenience? Wouldn't it make life easier when I was trying to juggle so much? But I couldn't ignore the question of what would be best for Maisie and her future. Surely the long-term benefits would outweigh any extra effort required. It struck me that I was caught up in my own inquiry of "why don't people do more". Why wasn't I making the step that I knew I should be making? I knew I had found the focus of my study. Understanding my own barriers to adopting environmental lifestyle choices was going to be crucial if I was ever to understand why others didn't do more. I also wanted to learn more about how I could best support people if they also chose to make sustainable lifestyle changes.

Staying focused on any other topic would have been almost impossible, but the all-too-regular reminders kept me on track. The research was not just about nappies, but on my personal decisions of when I did and didn't make eco-choices. I learnt about the small, subtle but essential steps that are needed to enable someone to make a lifestyle or behaviour change. The need for easy-to-understand language; having someone available to give assistance with decision-making and problem-solving; having support from those around you; and the importance of finding pride and joy in the changes being made. I also came to appreciate the deep relevance of social norms to an individual's behaviour. During my research, I spoke with a Somali mum who told me that were she in Somalia, where it is the norm to use cloth nappies, she would be using cloth, but as she was living in Bristol, she chose to use disposables just like those around her. To her, it was not a conscious decision, it was what she saw being done around her, no doubt reinforced by the free samples of baby products expectant mothers are given. Living my own inquiry ensured the research was real, tangible and personally valuable. Being awarded a distinction in my Master's degree encouraged me to pursue my passions and gave me confidence in my abilities as an adaptable change agent, able to act in whatever situation I may find myself in.

City life was less appealing with a small child. We wanted fewer late nights out with friends, and more laid-back places to go as a family. Our spare time was increasingly spent escaping with Maisie to the countryside for walks or camping. When Maisie developed asthma, with no real plans but a leap of faith, we moved to a small town on the Somerset-Devon border. It was such a treat to be back closer to nature. Every evening I took Maisie to the ponds at the end of the road to see the ducks and enjoy the changes in the hedges and trees.

Sometimes a leap into the unknown works out OK. The local college had a new post for someone to improve the sustainability of the campus. It was wonderful to join such a positive culture. Staff were energised, full of ideas and keen to get involved. The enthusiasm was refreshing and exciting and I was supported in trying out new ways to engage with staff and students. I had the familiar task of reducing resource use, whilst also working with the senior leadership as well as supporting curriculum managers. It was a fantastic position, but balancing this with a small child was tough. I look back, remembering the rush to get between nursery and work at the start and end of each day, the feelings of guilt for leaving Maisie at nursery, and the discomfort of arriving late to work, and leaving at spot-on five o'clock to pick her up before nursery closed.

When I was expecting Maisie's sister Tali, I set up my own business, *Action for Sustainability*, offering sustainability training, facilitation and consultancy. This is my chance to get involved with exciting projects with lots of organisations whilst also seeking some work-life balance. A lot of my work is based at home, writing documents, preparing workshops, and so on, with occasional meetings and days out running training programmes. I see more of the children that an employment could offer. It rarely works out super-smoothly and all-idyllic, but to me it's preferable to leaving them at nursery from 8am to 6pm five days a week. As ever there is no easy path. To get the balance I am seeking now – job satisfaction and a wholesome family life – takes hard and difficult internal negotiations and a lot of compromise.

I reflect on my journey so far, trying to find my place in the Great Turning and am content knowing that there is not just one place in which to make a difference. I look instead to being adaptable, and making best use of my skills to ensure I can have a positive influence, finding opportunities in whatever situations arise.

I reflect too, and appreciate the value of generational learning, from my own personal perspective of seeing my grandparents keeping a thermal flask by the kettle, always storing that spare bit of hot water for the next boil; heating the home by wood; gardening; breaking down old machine parts to reuse. I look at how my parents have built on this, bringing up their family with a vegetarian diet, subscribing to pressure groups, and recycling. We too are developing these initiatives, taking on the old ideas, and adding our own. I am as guilty as others for criticising past generations for leaving the world in a mess, but yet convinced that we can leave positive impacts too if our learning becomes the start point for our children.

I wonder where my activist-self is, and whether she is still on pause. I find her more present than ever in the professional self, and she is also very busy nurturing the future. Two very committed young girls are following fast in the footsteps, and keen to start where she left off, as this moment recently captured in my journal shows:

This morning was a non-uniform day for Maisie, the remit: dress as your favourite character from your favourite book in celebration of the new school library opening.

"What do you want to go as, Maisie?"

"Greenpeace."

"Oh, Emily from Dear Greenpeace?"

"No, Greenpeace."

So she gets dressed in some combats, my old Greenpeace t-shirt and a rainbow waistcoat. Looks good! Steve and I are still desperately trying to keep a link with books.

"Shall we find the Dear Greenpeace book so you can take it in?"

"No, I'm not Emily, I'm Greenpeace."

I have an idea.

"Would you like my special Greenpeace book with the pictures in of real Greenpeace activists?"

Maisie's face lights up (at last these dear parents have got it!).

I find the book – it is rather old, the Greenpeace story up to 1991. There are some stickers from an old campaign in there. I give one to Maisie and Tali to "complete" their outfits (Tali by this time has dressed in another old campaign t-shirt too!).

Maisie starts looking through the book. She is fascinated and asks questions about all the pictures. She sees a harpooned whale, and we talk about the picture of Greenpeace getting their inflatable boat in the way of moving the whale onto the factory ship. Steve and I talk about the vulnerability of Greenpeace activists in small boats in hostile situations. We explain to the girls how Greenpeace films the action, to "bear witness" and show the world what happens at sea.

Maisie notices another photo of a Greenpeace activist kneeling on a whale. She asks about it. The description says it is a calf that was killed – the Greenpeace activist is sitting with it while it dies.

"Does the whale like it sitting on him?" asks Maisie.

I say that I think the whale would appreciate the presence of a friend as it dies. We are looking at this. Tali (age three) says "I don't want it to die." Maisie agrees.

We continue to look, in silence, mourning the loss of the whale. It dawns on me that perhaps we have experienced a deep connection with the dying whale – we all felt the pain and sorrow through our interconnectedness. We felt the pain of the world through us.

I think back to when I was a child, looking at the pictures in the tree house. I connected with the animals in the images, and felt the pain and sorrow of the world through me. I didn't realise this was what was happening at the time, but looking back I see that it gave me strength and determination to stand up in defence of life on Earth.

I wish my girls well in their journeys.

3
How to Build a Lifeboat
Celia Sousek

"D'you know oil's going to run out some day, Dad?"

"Impossible."

"No, it's true. Look up Peak Oil on the Internet and see for yourself."

And although we did not know it at the time, this brief exchange between my seventeen year old son, Joe, and my husband, Paul, was going to set us on a path that would change our lives forever.

It was the beginning of December 2004. We had been living in a modest house, with a large garden, in semi-rural Kent near Sevenoaks for twenty years. Paul and I were in our mid fifties, and we had two sons – Ben, nineteen, in his second year at Plymouth University studying surf science and technology; and Joe, who was having a gap year before commencing his philosophy degree at Bristol University. Paul had started his own company in 1990 – a small market research agency specialising in Eastern Europe – and the business was successful enough to provide us with a reasonable living. In 2002 we'd divided our garden and built a bungalow large enough for all the family but which was designed to accommodate and facilitate Paul and I in our later years. We were secure, settled and comfortable. We thought nothing would change our way of life and we would live there forever. But Peak Oil changed all that.

Paul started researching and he soon became convinced that oil and other fossil fuels would inevitably run out. He learned that Peak Oil is the point in time when the maximum rate of petroleum extraction is reached, after which the rate of production enters terminal decline. By the 21st century life in the developed countries has become entirely dependent on the availability of cheap and plentiful fossil fuels. We rely on these for food, heating, lighting, transport, electronics – and everything else that makes up the modern world. Pessimistic predictions of future oil production were that either oil production was on the cusp of the peak, or it would occur shortly. Without a cheap and plentiful alternative source of energy, it would be impossible to maintain the modern way of living and the consequences would be devastating. Paul's predictions included stock market collapse, banking crises, long-term deep recessions, breakdown of retail distribution and perhaps even of law and order. In a word: chaos.

So what to do? Stick our heads in the sand, hope for the best and continue as normal or face the coming crisis head on?

Just before Christmas, Paul came up with his solution as to how our family would deal with the approaching energy crisis. We should build a "lifeboat" – a sustainable way of living with which to face the challenges of Peak Oil and climate change. We should sell up, move to the country, buy a farm, keep animals, grow our own food, use renewable energy and become as self-sufficient as possible. Did we have a happy Christmas – no we did not! I didn't want this. I was not prepared to leave my home, my way of life and my friends for an event that some people thought was so far in the future that it was not worth bothering about. I wanted to stay put. But it's not just about you and me, Paul argued, it's about Ben and Joe and their future too.

So over the next few weeks, having listened to Paul's arguments, in particular that market research would be one of the first business services to suffer in the event of economic downturn, I was persuaded to join Paul, albeit very reluctantly, to look into the possibility of buying a farm. I knew this dramatic change might be achievable because Paul had already started a new life once before. Born in Prague in 1951, he left Czechoslovakia when the Russians invaded in 1968 and came alone to England. By the time we met in 1981 he was a director in a market research company and owned a flat. It was only after the Velvet Revolution in 1990 that he was able to visit Prague.

Obviously this drastic change of lifestyle would have the greatest effect on Paul and myself since the boys would continue with their university education. But we all decided that if we were going to make such a change, we should move to Cornwall where hopefully farms would be cheaper – it would be impossible for us to afford a farm in Kent – and, Paul reasoned, there was plenty of wind for a wind turbine and sun for solar panels that would be essential for our new way of life! Both boys were happy with this idea. Ben was determined to work in the surfing industry so having his family home in Cornwall was ideal, and although Joe would probably work in London, he loved the county where we had enjoyed many holidays.

The trouble was we knew nothing about farming. How much land would we need? What animals would we keep? How do you actually look after farm animals and farmland? Would we get any farming subsidies? There was so much we didn't know but, nevertheless, Paul and I started our search. We began by excluding parts of Cornwall – the industrial china clay country around St Austell, the old mining areas of Cambourne and

Redruth, and West Cornwall, near Penzance, simply because it was so remote. We ended up with North and South Cornwall where the relief, climate and soil type are only really suitable for rearing livestock – few arable crops are grown. We registered with estate agents there dealing with agricultural properties. We immediately received details of so many farms for sale that it became obvious that we were considering buying a farm at the very time that many farmers were leaving farming because of the introduction of the new EEC Single Farm Payment. If experienced farmers were leaving farming, was this the time for newcomers to enter the industry, I argued? All the more choice said Paul, so we made appointments to view four farms and set off.

The first farm we saw had about ten acres of land, a derelict farmhouse and a few ramshackle buildings – it was awful. But we did start talking to the neighbouring farmer about our plans and he then invited us to see his herd of North Devon cattle, known as Red Rubies because of the colour of their coats. He told us they were smaller than most beef cattle, were docile and handled well, calved easily, produced excellent marbled beef and "do well on a bramble". They looked wonderful and we suddenly realised that these could be the cattle for us. He was so kind and encouraging – saying "I likes the look of thee, m'dears" – that even I started to become more enthusiastic.

At this point, we had an amazing stroke of luck. I was reading a magazine in a Sevenoaks coffee shop when I found an article about a London couple who'd sold their business, bought a farm in Sussex, and were keeping a herd of beef cattle and operating a meat box scheme as a way of adding value to their beef. And they were going to run a course called "Cows for Beginners" in ten days' time. So I booked us both on the course. It was excellent and by the end we'd learnt all the basics – theoretical at least – about keeping beef cattle and how much land we would need per animal. We had also met other crazy people with similar plans as ours which was enormously encouraging, and I finally accepted that we were actually going to buy a farm. When we told our friends, half said we were mad and half that we were brave, but I preferred mad since brave made it sound far too serious an undertaking.

We sold our house and in April 2005, after looking at many properties, we found Cottage Farm, a sixty-five acre farm in Jacobstow about four miles from Crackington Haven on the beautiful North Cornwall coast. This was the first farm that fulfilled all our requirements and luckily our offer proved sufficient and was accepted. We transferred our combined modest pension pot into a new, hurriedly set up self-administered pension scheme, which then purchased part of the farmland. Paul thought that pension funds would in any case start collapsing with the rest of the financial system, so investing our pension pot in agricultural land seemed much safer.

Paul, Ben and I moved in at the beginning of a very hot August – Joe was now travelling in SE Asia. The previous owner was leaving farming so we bought the tractor (the ultimate boy's toy for Paul), the quad-bike, most of the other machinery, a flock of sixty Suffolk sheep and a delinquent farm dog (he came free but soon went back to the previous owner).

We began by introducing ourselves to our neighbours, a family of dairy farmers. They seemed surprised when we said we were completely new to farming and intended to keep Red Rubies, but from the start they were unfailingly generous with their time and advice and it will never be possible for us to repay the debt we owe them. From them we have learnt most of the practical aspects of farming – how to deal with difficult lambing and calving and to treat twin-lamb disease, fly strike and foot-rot – and, much to their delight, they had to pull Paul and his tractor out of the mud on several occasions during our first months, and no doubt had a good laugh about it in the pub. They also kept a Red Ruby bull as their herd bull and agreed to sell us their Ruby cross-calves rather than sell them at market.

During the first week, I got to grips with the Rural Payments Agency on the administrative aspects of acquiring a farm. The holding number, unique to each farm, had to be transferred to us and this had to happen before we could register for the new Single Farm Payment. If we didn't register by a particular date, we would never get the SFP, which would be disastrous to our financial planning. The RPA, a new organisation set up to handle the SFP, was experiencing problems with its computer system to the extent that our farm completely disappeared from its records for about a month. With the SFP deadline rapidly approaching, I spent whole days on the phone and was reduced to tears before our farm was finally "found" again just in time to register for the SFP.

We'd been told that sheep are only happy when they are escaping or dying, and if they can die escaping then they're really happy. Nevertheless we decided to keep forty of them. We bought some chickens and geese too, and started buying calves from our neighbours. They were only a few days old when we got them and were ideal because if they didn't go where we wanted we could simply pick them up. They were bucket fed with formula milk until fully weaned at three months. Within twenty-eight days of birth calves have to be registered with the British Cattle Movement Service, which allocates each a numbered passport. But we also gave them all names. Early on we decided where we'd have our vegetable plot and bought two pigs that cleared the nettles, brambles and docks, fertilising the ground as they worked, before ending up in our freezer – they were rather aggressive, always trying to bite us, so this was not a problem. Another neighbour shot one of the pigs for us, then cleaned and butchered it to teach us how it's done – the second one we did on our own.

One of my main concerns about moving to Cornwall was that we knew absolutely no one in the area and that being "incomers" it would take years before we made any friends. But I was completely wrong. Everyone was very welcoming and within weeks we were getting to know people and made good friends among both the farming community and other incomers. September was beautiful but October brought the start of the autumn gales when we experienced horizontal driving rain for the first time, and knee-deep mud. Suddenly farming wasn't quite so much fun.

We started lambing in March. Naively we thought that lambs were born and they then got up, suckled and started hopping about; but not so. Suffolk sheep have been bred intensively to produce a good meat carcass but in the process many ewes have lost some of the mothering instinct and some lambs have little will to live. Several lambs died – we felt absolutely awful – until in despair we decided to milk each ewe so that we could bottle-feed their lambs with the colostrum, which is essential for survival. So we had to try to be present at every birth, which meant taking it in turns to get up in the night (when most lambs are born) for the next three weeks until lambing ended. We also had to intervene with several difficult births, some of which resulted in dead lambs. We'd been told that if you have livestock, you also have dead stock but we knew our inexperience and ignorance contributed to the dead lambs.

As summer approached the ewes had to be sheared and Paul decided to do this himself – a big mistake since he could hardly stand upright for a week afterwards. He also had to deal with foot rot and fly strike. Keeping sheep was proving to be hard work.

During the first year we decided to go into a two year organic conversion with Organic Farmers & Growers. We also changed our breed of sheep to Wiltshire Horn, an old native breed that sheds its short fleece – no need for shearing – and is less susceptible to fly-strike which makes it great for organic farming, since we're not allowed to use preventative medical treatments. The Wiltshire Horn ewes are good mothers, the lambs robust and we've had none of the disturbed nights and problems encountered with the Suffolks.

We kept our first Ruby cross-heifers as the basis of our herd, but the bullocks had to be sent to the abattoir by the age of thirty months. This was very hard to do since we'd raised these calves virtually from birth, but they had to go and we consoled ourselves by knowing that we'd done our best to give these animals as good a life as possible. We're lucky in having a small farmers' abattoir nearby which greatly reduces stress for

41

our animals. We introduced a beef and lamb meat box scheme under the name of Cottage Farm Organics to add value to our produce –fresh organic meat sustainably farmed so it doesn't cost the Earth. This started slowly but we advertise locally and on various websites and we now have many regular customers nationwide. In addition, we also sell our produce at local farmers' markets and agricultural shows.

The same year we bought our first adult cows and a pedigree bull and have gradually established our own suckler herd of organic Red Rubies where the calves remain with the herd, able to suckle until eight months old. They all look wonderful in the sun, their rich red coats contrasting with the lush green pasture – it's lush because we do have lots of rain in Cornwall. My favourite sight on the farm is a newborn calf with tiny, pearly white hooves that only change colour when it first stands.

In the second year we had a borehole drilled to reduce the very large water bills we had to pay, largely due to the cows drinking so much. We approached two companies and when they both sent in their water diviners we were somewhat sceptical, particularly Paul. The first diviner – the third generation of his family to have this gift – also had a PhD in hydrology. Holding his dousing rods lightly in his fingers, he started walking purposely over our "wet" field and his rods led to a spot where he claimed two underground streams crossed. The second, a rather fey, ethereal woman, tripping lightly around, surprisingly found no water in the same field and her rods led to the next field. We decided to back the PhD and his drilling team proved him right since there they found a "gusher" – enough water for three hundred cows – to serve the house, the drinkers in the covered yard and all the troughs in the fields. This cost us about £8000 but reduced our water bill from £1800 pa to about £100 pa so by now it has more than paid for itself.

Since then we have also gradually converted to renewable energy. We have installed solar thermal panels, a wood burning stove with a back boiler and a heat store to provide hot water; photovoltaic panels and a wind turbine to produce electricity; a thirty-year-old reconditioned wood-burning Rayburn in the kitchen for heating and cooking; and we make our own bio-diesel from waste vegetable oil, which we use to fuel the tractor, Land Rover and car for local deliveries of our meat boxes. The two acres of woodland on the farm, together with our overgrown hedgerows, make us already self-sufficient in wood, although we have planted over a hundred additional trees for future coppicing.

As a result of all this and after a great deal of draft-proofing and insulating we are 'carbon positive' as measured by the Cornwall Sustainable Building Trust: we have cut almost all our CO2 emissions and in addition generate clean electricity for our neighbours. We were also the first house in Cornwall to be designated as a low-carbon, low-energy dwelling by SuperHomes, a charity that aims to demonstrate how existing houses can be so converted, something that will be essential for the whole of the UK housing stock. To promote these ideals we hold open days every month from April to October that offer practical hands-on advice on how to reduce dependence on high-cost fossil fuel energy as well as sharing our accumulated knowledge of new organic and permaculture farming practices.

Paul has also become very active in the Transition movement and runs the Transition North Cornwall website, and he's also joined the Tamar Valley Organic Group of progressive farmers. As a result of all his activities, he has been invited to give presentations on renewable energy and transition farming to the Royal Agricultural College, a cross-party committee of MPs in the House of Commons, the Eco-Innovations Conference in Westminster and at various other conferences. In November 2011 Paul's efforts to farm in a sustainable way were recognised when he was runner up in the BBC's Food and Farming Awards "Sustainable Farmer of the Year" category. And in December Cottage Farm was "Highly Commended" in the Low Carbon Business category of the Cornwall Sustainability Awards.

Taking up farming has not been easy. We are always short of money; we have to buy second-hand equipment and farm machinery, and are always looking to barter. We've experienced many difficulties with livestock and weather. There was the first case of fly strike when the sheep eventually died. One of the first heifers we bought – too young to give birth – was, unknown to us, already pregnant and we found her one morning with a half-born dead calf. It was so big she'd dislocated her hind leg and had to be shot. Then a cow in labour had torsion of the uterus, when the uterus had rotated 360 degrees so that the calf couldn't be born. Amazingly the vet put his arm inside the cow and rotated the uterus back again, and both the cow and calf survived. We've also had a mass breakout when our entire herd escaped on to the lane, with Paul in pursuit on the quad, while I had to enlist passing motorists to help get them back in the field.

The problems did not stop with the animals, either. Our first wind turbine blew to pieces in an autumn gale. Rather than have a British wind turbine installed, Paul decided after considerable research to import one directly from China for a third of the cost. We had it installed and everything was fine until the gale. From the way the support pole had fractured it appeared there was a manufacturing fault so we sent photographs to the Chinese company and requested a replacement. Would we ever hear from them again? Yes – they agreed with our conclusion and sent a new turbine. Just before last Christmas a lightning strike took out our telephone, broadband, computer systems, and all our renewable energy equipment.

I was in my office when the lightning struck, which caused a power surge to blow covers and cables off the fuse boxes, terminals and inverters that are housed there; a mug of coffee on my desk to explode; and sparks and smoke to fill the room setting off the alarms. It was weeks before we got back to normal and seven months to settle our insurance claim. And this summer we've lost a whole field of silage – over a hundred bales of our winter feed – to rain.

As you can imagine, living here we have become much more aware of the weather, the seasons and the natural world around us. Spring brings lambing and calving, primroses and violets in the Cornish hedges and the buzzards nesting in our wood. With summer come the swallows returning to the same nests year after year, the smell of mown grass as farmers race to make hay and silage before it rains, hares in our meadows and, inevitably, foxes with cubs raiding our free range chickens and geese. In early autumn, as the leaves begin to turn, the swallows gradually congregate on the telephone wires and suddenly they've gone only to be replaced by starlings in winter, flocking in great black clouds before settling to roost for the night. On winter nights we load up the wood burner, draw the curtains and, if we do look outside, there's not a light to be seen anywhere and the only sounds we hear are owls hooting, and foxes calling to each other.

We will have been here for seven years soon – the time has flown by although the pace of life is so much slower. Cottage Farm is now our home and, despite my initial misgivings and the various problems we continue to experience, there's no way that I would return to our old life. I love it here even though it's hard work. Ben, as he hoped, is working in the surfing industry in Newquay and is now married to Caroline; they are expecting their first child. Joe is living in London. After working with asylum seekers for the UK Border Agency he is now, very appropriately, working in the Department of Energy and Climate Change in Whitehall – Paul is delighted that he now has a man inside the ministry.

We do not regret our change in lifestyle. Since we arrived in Cornwall energy prices have continued to rise, we have experienced the first oil shock due to geological rather than political causes in 2008, and it appears that conventional oil peaked in 2006 and there is uncertainty over the security of remaining oil and gas supplies. All this is causing the worldwide economic slowdown and contributing to the bankers' crisis; and now the Euro looks to be on the point of collapse, if not the whole world financial system. At some point the current way of life may disintegrate, including security. It will then be necessary for everyone wherever they live to decide how to face these difficulties. Some argue that large cities are more sustainable than rural areas. Many will choose to remain in cities and suburbs and meet the problems in familiar surroundings. Others, like us, will move to the country and work in the much more labour-intensive agriculture of the future. Here our farm is already part of a close-knit community where we are mutually dependent on each other, particularly in times of trouble. The emergence of the Transition Movement, with its emphasis on local resilience and sustainability, has helped to focus people's attention on the problems to come and on exploring the various ways of helping each other.

Meanwhile farming has become more profitable and farmland has doubled in price. But whatever some people may think, it is not necessary to be rich to do what we're trying to do. Being in the fortunate position to swap an overpriced house in a large city for a country smallholding takes you a long way towards resilient sustainability. Co-housing in eco-friendly communities offers an even more affordable way to escape city life. Since we moved here we've made many acquaintances, both young and old, building other lifeboats and none of us belong to the privileged few. I'd say it's more an attitude of mind, a belief that it is possible to adapt to a new way of life and learn fresh skills. This change may be forced on many people later – we've chosen to do it early, before the forces of collapse overwhelm the current way of life.

As a result, we're on our way to achieving what we set out to do – we are building our lifeboat. We are now living in a sustainable and resilient way, helping our community to be as self-sufficient as possible and trying to persuade others that they too can change. Where we can, we barter – our beef, lamb and eggs for milk, venison, pork and vegetables. Paul and I hope that by moving to Cottage Farm and taking up farming we are offering our sons and extended family the possibility of a sustainable future in the difficult days that may come. Perhaps, after all and in spite of the mass of evidence to the contrary, there may be a way for humans to live on this planet without ruining it.

4
Knickers to That!
Emma Kidd

I was born in 1981, and had a modest upbringing, growing up in a small market town in the UK in the middle of the capitalist boom, which I was largely sheltered from due to my love of the outdoors and disinterest in modern popular childhood crazes such as boy bands and shopping. There have since been two main themes in my life journey so far. The first is an intense, prolonged discomfort with the status quo presented to me as a young woman growing up in the 21st Century – for the lack of humanness, compassion and meaning in the systems and organisations that have been created, and their tendency toward destruction and exploitation. The second is my growing sense of wonder and reverence for the dynamic web of life on Earth, and a strong intuition of how this is intrinsically, and necessarily, linked to the practice of sustainability. It is these themes that I will weave together in recounting my experience of bringing a more responsible, sustainable and beneficial way of being into practice through my ethical underwear project, Emiliana Underwear.

When I was growing up I never had an interest in fashion, and still don't. I have never bought into the idea that style should be dictated. However, I have always had a love of colour and textiles, drawing and creating – and have also had the ability to perceive quality, in fabrics and clothing, since a very young age, despite not being particularly interested in shopping. I have also always loved underwear, ever since my grandmother bought me my first matching cotton vest and knicker set. So after studying art and textiles for two years at an art school, I then trained as a lingerie designer at De Montfort University in Leicester, England – the only university in the world at that time to teach underwear design and manufacture to degree level. After graduating, at the age of 21, I was given my first job in Hong Kong. I left the UK to move there in May 2003, which happened to be during a nasty flu-type epidemic – SARS (Severe Acute Respiratory Syndrome). I remember that the aeroplane was only half full, and most of those on board were wearing face masks. Despite this, I was not scared – it was my first job, not just as any designer, but an international designer working with multinational brands in countries all over the world. I was 21, and the opportunity to move to Hong Kong and to build a career in Asia was beyond my wildest dreams, especially since I had never before travelled outside of Europe.

On one level, life and work for me in Hong Kong was exciting, fast and fun. I enjoyed many corporate and ex-pat "luxuries": socialising with colleagues, taking clients to Michelin-starred restaurants and charging bottles of vintage Champagne to my company credit card. Outside of work, Hong Kong and South East Asia were exciting areas to explore, geographically and culturally. On weekends I went hiking in the National Parks; body boarding at one of the numerous beaches; and took boat trips with friends to explore this fascinating archipelago, stopping often to dive into the cool depths of the South China Sea. I searched for tiny, hidden local restaurants in a quest for the best Cantonese dim-sum or Malaysian laksa noodles. These excursions in nature and culture were part of what kept me in Hong Kong for 5 years, for on another level I found this life lonely, destructive and superficial. I experienced the coldness and destruction that capitalism and consumerism leave in their wake; the feelings they create of never having enough, never being good enough, never being satisfied. I also witnessed the reality of the social and environmental destruction caused by their industrial processes in China.

Everywhere I turned, at work, on the streets of Hong Kong, in conversations with friends, I came face-to-face with the foundation stone of capitalism – quantification – that reduces everything to that which can be separated, measured, and assigned a numerical, financial, value. It stripped the qualities, dynamism and sacredness out of life, and led to a lack of compassion and humanness on many levels of my everyday experience. This was played out in many different aspects of my life. In the design work that I was involved in at work, quality was constantly undermined by the bottom line. The stress of working in high-pressure environments was constantly visible on friends' faces, from always having to meet higher targets and further increase sales, orders and profit; this led some to alcohol and drug abuse. The machinists sewing the garments in the factories that I visited in China were treated like robots, being given mindless tasks to repeat constantly for hours on end, and never referred to by name but instead assigned a number. The bustling streets of Hong Kong Island would heave daily, rain or shine, always active 24/7, yet people rarely had time to stop and chat, or to take much notice of their surroundings. I was lonely, and felt extremely isolated, even though I was one in seven million. In my apartment I would sit and imagine all of the people in all of the skyscrapers in Hong Kong as best I could, then I would dissolve the walls so that I could see the density of these people, so close in proximity, yet so separate from each other in their minds and their lives. I felt the weight of this collective separation as if it sat directly on my shoulders.

The suffering I experienced stemmed from a deep, societal malaise, but when living in the middle of it it was pretty hard to get a vantage point on it. It just consumed me. The initial design work that I was engaged in for large retail clients when I first moved to Hong Kong I nicknamed "paint by numbers", and the "McDonalds" of design. Unless the design was for a luxury brand or market leader, we just had to choose underwear shapes that had already been made, change the colour and fabric, and add or take away a bow or some lace. There was no meaningful designing for us to be engaged in because the buyers just wanted styles that had already previously sold well, or were selling well for other brands. Not only was there no desire for originality or creativity, there was no assessment of what the end customer really wanted, or would benefit from and, at that time, aside from general national regulations, there was certainly no consideration as to whether any of the manufacturing or sourcing processes were environmentally or socially responsible.

Working in the "fashion industry", and living in Hong Kong, I also experienced the consumer side of this process. There was row upon row of air conditioned shopping malls filling the already dense urban spaces, touting a massive array of garments, which even then will have mostly been made in China. There were gigantic billboards plastered around the city visually instructing women on how they "should" look – which in Hong Kong is always thinner, and with ever-whiter skin. This whole city was set up for "consumers", not people for whom these retailers were providing a service. To me these retailers felt more like drug dealers, providing the means for a manufactured social addiction and social climbing. However, it is all just a huge trick; those companies needed us to survive, to keep making a profit – they were not feeding us, we were feeding them – a clever, painstakingly executed illusion. They played on peoples' insecurities, desires for acceptance and a need to conform, so that the organisations and corporations could sustain themselves, and their insatiable hunger for profit.

Looking back I quite quickly became depressed and my sense of self-worth plummeted. Money did not make me happy, buying things did not make me happy and nor did success. I began to hate the way I looked and became very body conscious; I felt oversized and unattractive. I dated men that I was totally incompatible with because I didn't believe that I deserved any better. I also became ill frequently and constantly suffered from digestive problems and fatigue. It felt like something deep inside me couldn't cope anymore and just shut down. I lost my spark, my joie de vivre. I started becoming more of a recluse, socialising became a chore and I retreated more and more into myself. I realised that I wanted more from life, so I took a break and left Hong Kong for four months to go travelling around South America. For my life in Hong Kong this marked the start of the end. I returned from an amazing, mind-expanding and fulfilling travelling experience, to a new job in an even more suffocating, controlled work environment than I had previously experienced, and so in my last year of living in Hong Kong I suffered a kind of anxiety that left me unable to even carry out my work. I couldn't do my "job", and to my disbelief I was put on probation. I had experienced a rising career with leaps of promotion, fast on my way to becoming Head of Design or Design Director if I had stayed on track – yet, I found that I couldn't even carry out simple tasks that were put in front of me. I just didn't care about my work or profession anymore and so everything became a huge effort. The design work I did felt completely meaningless and so it became a physical battle to even put pen to paper. I missed deadlines, and my work lacked interest and effort. However, none of my actions were calculated or explicitly directed as an act of rebellion; the suffering was more subtle, deeper and pervasive than that. The lack of humanness and meaning, that I could feel and see all around me, had gradually become too much for my mind and body to cope with. I had to leave.

What happened next was that I had my whole world shaken up and down – in a good way. I made a giant leap into the unknown; I left my job, my apartment, my career and flew back to the UK. I discovered that a place where people were asking the same questions as me actually exists! I had stumbled upon an advert for Schumacher College, an International College for Sustainability and Ecology in Devon, England, just before leaving Hong Kong, and made my way straight there to participate in two residential short courses that were entitled, "Can the Earth Survive Capitalism?" and "Designing for Sustainability". Later that year I took the bigger step and moved on site for seven months to join the Master's degree in Holistic Science. And whoosh – a whole new way of seeing emerged.

Suddenly I was being presented with scientific, practical and philosophical stories of life that were dynamic and interactive, imbued with meaning and creativity, chaos and complexity – stories that made sense and felt right. For the first time in my life I felt that the Earth was alive! I became able to see the dynamism in plants, eco-systems and in life in general. I learned not just intuitively, but also intellectually, how the whole is always in relation to, not separate from, the parts, whether in a human being, a plant or a complex Earth system such as the carbon cycle. I had been renewed with a sense of awe and wonder for life.

I have always believed in equality and respect, for humans and the environment – but my experience at Schumacher added a belief of the need for reverence also. Suddenly the methods of quantification that capitalism and mass production use to measure and "value" life felt even more out of place. I realised that in our society of conspicuous "consumption" we not only disrespect life but we also deny its reverence so that we can justify exploiting it for profit. I needed to try something different, I just did not want to be a part of this anymore.

However, after graduating I was unemployed, with a large bank loan owing for my Master's degree, no money coming in and so in quite a state of financial despair. I had all of these new and wonderful insights into how we could right some of our terrible wrongs in the world, but I felt that, outside of Schumacher College or close friends, no-one could hear me, or wanted to listen. So I started connecting to smaller projects where people were fighting for their values and also struggling financially, but who were at least walking their talk. One of which was Whomadeyourpants? an ethical underwear cooperative based in south England who work with refugee women, and who I still design for today. They are not afraid to challenge the systems that they disagree with, and even dare to see "responsible" business practice as "normal". This gave me hope, fulfilment and a renewed energy to keep going. These projects sustained me emotionally, and intellectually, but not financially. So, I moved back in with my family. I was sat at home, unemployed, with no money even to travel, let alone to invest in my ideas but with a determination that just would not rest.

Then I had my big idea. It was a bright sunny day in late summer and what came to me in a flash of clarity and inspiration was that I just had to start. I could manifest my way of seeing the world by living it in a practical way. I could begin to create work for myself making sustainable lingerie, by doing what I already knew how to do, from exactly where I was, in that place, in that moment. By then I had over eight years of industry experience in professional lingerie design and development, and I had been dreaming about what a sustainable version of these processes and products would look like since my very first year in Hong Kong, always creating various ideas for ethical projects but never feeling happy about one part or another. With my long held obsession over the needless, endlessly increasing supplies of "stuff" in the world, I wasn't happy just sourcing materials that pertained to be "eco-friendly". I felt so strongly that we have already created enough "stuff", already more than the Earth can handle. So, if we already have all of this "stuff", why not use some of that? Why not turn our unwanted materials into something new? This all came together into a kind of "a-ha" moment. I had a pile of unwanted stretchy t-shirts and tops in my drawers, and what is stretchy material perfect for? Knickers! And so, in a flash, started my responsible knicker revolution with my upcycling project, Emiliana Underwear.

The overall idea of Emiliana is to show women that they can be flexible and creative with how they fulfil their need for underwear, without compromising the needs of other people, or the environment, by upcycling unwanted clothing and fabrics. Instead of designing for profit, or for some external "consumer", I started by trying to create a pair of knickers that I would love to wear, and that I would also love to make. I only had a domestic sewing machine at home, so I wanted them to be simple to sew but to still look professional and fit perfectly. I came up with a simple shorts design, and started out by just making knickers for friends, and by Christmas time I was making them for friends of friends and then also sharing my insights and experiences on a blog that I created for the project. The following year I was invited to sell at a large women's conference in London called Women on Fire, and I also started to sell on markets, in small boutiques and online stores.

Each piece of Emiliana Underwear is unique, and the fabrics, design and fit have been given a degree of thought and attention, not to mention love, that just does not exist in the mass-produced goods available in our high street stores. They are also upcycled. I chose to upcycle clothing rather than use new eco-fabrics because I understood the complexities of the situation. For example, organic cotton means a hell of lot more water is being wasted, and natural yarns used to create stretch jersey fabrics are still incredibly energy-intensive. I source unwanted fabrics and clothing, mostly from charity shops in the UK, and so any money I do spend on fabrics goes to a worthy, not-for-profit cause. This gives the clothes a new lease of life, and gives the Earth, and people, a rest from yet more resource extraction and production.

When I started I did not know where this project would go but I knew instinctively that I just had to trust in the process, and that the most valuable learning comes through doing. For me it was the process that was more valuable than the knickers themselves; they were a beautiful token to my action of challenging systems that I disagreed with. After a few months I also decided to create a make-your-own knickers kit as a way to share that process. I also found sewing and preparing the kits alone at home quite lonely and so I searched for ways to connect with women directly. I started to lead knicker-making workshops, and to give talks on upcycling, teaching women how to make their own knickers and upcycle their own clothing. I find these activities much more enjoyable and rewarding, rather than just being a producer of goods.

Emiliana enables me to sustain a small livelihood that I can live and create on my own terms. I feel that the value Emiliana holds for other women is in enabling them to satisfy their need for underwear based on values, relationships and co-learning. So Emiliana is not only sustainable, it is also empowering. The knickers are achievable on minimal sewing experience, on any domestic sewing machine that has a zigzag stitch. This process enables women to use and develop their practical and creative abilities, to satisfy their own wants and needs, instead of relying on a commercial system to do it for them. The skill of making up the knickers is a replicable process, and once they have copied the fabric pattern onto paper they can repeat it as many times as they like, giving them the chance to upcycle unwanted materials, which means saving them from the waste stream, and giving them a new lease of life. This has a broader level of value too: reducing people's reliance on mass-produced goods reduces their connection to purely for-profit based organisations and economies that are accountable only to shareholders, and creates creative, local solutions to resource and waste management. I am also experimenting with a new open-sourcing policy of sharing the patterns to local community groups of women, in return for information on their project to share on the Emiliana website. I am currently trialling this with a friend in Mexico who is taking the patterns to different groups of women to see how it can support their need for underwear, and possibly their need for financial income.

With Emiliana I try to demonstrate the possibility for the dissemination of practical knowledge which usually stays locked within our educational or commercial institutions, and to dispel the illusions around mass-made clothing. Both keep many women disempowered by feeling that they will never achieve a decent alternative to options on the high street. Beyond just being a small part of a solution to exploitation and waste, Emiliana can empower other women to create their own solutions; to rekindle or enliven their creativity and ability to create; and not least to realise the power that they hold in the decision of "to buy" or "not to buy", and the responsibility of the long list of processes, whether harmful or helpful, that those decisions carry.

At this point in time, a large barrier to women making their own underwear is a lack of time. Women who work full-time often have little time for themselves, let alone time to hand-make things. From my own experience being self-employed, I find it hard to believe that we can make the most sustainable choices for life when we do work full time. So there are big, complex questions around lifestyle choice and financial constraints that are involved if women want to make the time to hand-make more of what they want or need themselves. Another challenge that I have experienced is that I have not been successful in getting many of the ready-made knickers to sell in stores because of the low cost-price that the retailers demand. They usually charge customers more than double the amount that the producer receives. For me to accurately reflect my costs in the price that I charge the retailer, the knickers would end up being a very high-end luxury product that few could afford, which is not what I want.

I really enjoy sharing my knowledge and upcycling experience with other women, but in the face of our current social and environmental crises, it does not feel enough. Emiliana enables us to directly make use of what we have already created, our unwanted clothing, which is great and much needed. What it cannot do so directly is give people the lived experience necessary to develop an understanding of the dynamic, interconnected nature of nature, so that they feel an intrinsic part of the web of life on Earth, not separate from it. This is exactly what I think is needed to understand that, to be sustainable, we need to collectively work with nature in every decision concerning all of our designs, resource use, and production processes.

When I am in my back garden on a clear night I look up at the stars and think wow, life really is a miracle. We live on a ball of rock, with a furnace for a belly, spinning around a much larger fireball called the Sun, in the depths of some mostly unknown, vast dimension called "space". We have developed theories and stories to explain these mysteries of the Universe and of life on Earth, but so far the majority tell us that we are separate from both. Then I take a breath, and take time to really think about how many parts of the systems on this Earth and in this universe have contributed toward supporting just that one breath. I contemplate the "known", and the as-yet unknown, and then I instinctively understand just how interconnected, complex and mysterious it all is. For me the world is then inherently imbued with meaning and creativity, and I am filled with awe and with wonder.

To achieve my current way of seeing life, and my place in it, as I have described above, I have had to step aside from the status quo, question many taken-for-granted assumptions that western life and society is based on, and learn to think and experience life directly for myself again, outside of the constraints of mainstream theories and beliefs. I have had to alter my perception to start to explore life outside of the capitalist, mechanistic "reality" that we have created, so that I can start to work on a different "reality" that benefits all; where everything is connected, where the part is no more or less important than the whole, and where the health of the relationships between the parts is just as important as the parts themselves, just as it is in the Earth's eco-systems. I feel that for us to be sustainable, it is necessary for the individual and the collective to also do this. It is the opening of hearts and minds that allows us to experience the wonder and awe of our dynamic living planet and our place in it, and to appreciate the qualities of life, not just quantities, and then let this be reflected in our actions. This opening can generate a deep and meaningful respect and reverence for all life, which then naturally calls forth other qualities of life such as celebration, wonder and mystery. It is this sense of deep connection, of awe and of wonder, of curiosity and celebration, that I feel are essential for us to develop, as a human race, if we are to not only survive on this Earth, and "sustain" our race, but also learn how to thrive.

5
Material Girl Sees the Flaw
Christine Bone

It all started at the photocopying machine.

As a course administrator, part of my job was to copy and send out the pre-reading packs before each workshop. With little else to do whilst waiting I would find myself perusing articles I would never have thought to read. Topics like eco-feminism, Gaia and social constructionism started to enter my awareness – what on earth was that about? Little did I know that this bewilderment would turn into a thirst for knowledge about the state of our planet that has never been quenched since. Over the years, Greenham Common and a few other events had crossed my consciousness but in those days I was preoccupied with raising three boys, leaving me with little time to take much notice of either feminism or the environment. Now, as I stood by the photocopier reading this new material, I felt shivers down my spine.

The dormant seed of ecological awareness began to germinate. Perhaps we all have this within us if the right conditions are present. As I progressed from this casual reading to taking the books home, my interest began to grow and I was surprised to find myself deeply engaged in this new theoretical understanding of the world. I read the work of Berry, Macy, Capra, and Reason: here were people who believed in the interconnectedness of all things, which resonated deeply with my own thoughts and life experiences. Thus began my environmental awakening.

You see, at this point I was the classic "Material Girl". I have always loved fashion, clothes, dressing up, interior design, the arts, and to this end always wanted things, and lots of them. Well, at least I thought I did. I read all those women's magazines that promised me that, if only I bought the right clothes, shoes or a "must have" designer bag, I would become happy with who I was. But it never quite delivered, there was always something even more desirable twinkling from the pages, saying to me "Come on you really need this, think of the difference it will make," so I kept on buying. Don't get me wrong, I wasn't totally unaware; I had always had a social conscience and had been involved in lots of volunteering and charitable work in the past, but for me shopping was a passion. I was a certified shopaholic!

I had returned recently to England with my family after spending the previous two decades in Hong Kong, the USA and Paris. In Hong Kong I had shopped in the factory outlets where clothes were very cheap. I often bought as much as I could carry, loading myself down with bags that then had to be carried on the underground and then bus. I would be brimming over with the success of buying so many bargains, so many that a few would never be worn. In Paris it was the chic style that appealed. As the wife of a successful businessman, I was convinced I had to look the part. However, for all the material success we had achieved as a family, I felt that something was missing. Soon I found myself back in the UK and in need of a job that would give me some measure of fulfilment.

I applied for only one position and luckily I was accepted – or was it fate? Perhaps that little seed was already there and just needed the time and space to grow.

I found myself in the right place at the right time. My new job at the University of Bath was Course Administrator for the MSc in Responsibility and Business Practice. What made this course different was that it encouraged students to follow their own paths of study towards a world where environmental sustainability and social justice would become prime considerations for business. A heady requisite, I now realise.

I began to feel compelled to join the course but I was now well into middle age and, having left school at sixteen, tertiary education seemed daunting, steeped in ivory towers. I was very fearful of failure and wondered if I would even be accepted for, let alone complete, the two year course.

A year later, after much further reading and an application paper, I, along with thirty-two others, began a course of study that was to change me in a way I could never have imagined at the time.

Consumerism

For the first time I became aware of a number of unsettling facts concerning the future of our species: if the number of humans on this planet continues to rise as expected there will be nine billion of us by 2050; we risk running out of not just oil but many other of the vital resources and services that keep this biosphere alive. If everyone in the world had my ecological footprint we would need three fresh Earths to sustain us all. And if everyone lived to the USA's standard we would need five planets[1]. When one considers our overuse of the world's limited resources and our current inability to recycle the major part of our waste, one can only realise that unless we drastically cut our consumption, we are on course for irreversible environmental damage, resource wars and possibly social and economic meltdown. The developing world is likely to be the first to suffer, and has little power to avoid catastrophe. Perhaps we can already see the first stages of this process, as disasters come first to those who have the least power to survive them.

How could I not do something? I started by doing the normal environmental things like recycling, buying local food or fair trade where possible, reducing my use of chemical cleaners and other products. I changed my car for one with low carbon emissions. I even reduced my use of water and the washing of clothes, yet I still seemed only to be scraping the surface. I felt obliged to examine my need to consume.

Surely buying clothes made in the developing world was helpful? I had certainly assumed that it must be good for the economy in these countries. That's what our accepted model dictates: as long as we have economic growth, everyone's standard of living improves. I thought that the more I bought, the better the lives of the poorest would be; and that naive thought had buoyed up my purchasing power.

There is no doubt that globalisation has drawn millions of people into paid employment across the developing world. At the end of the supply chain, their work is fuelling the growth in national exports. Their jobs should be providing them with income, security and the support needed to lift them out of poverty. Instead, according to an Oxfam report, these workers, often females, are systematically being denied their fair share of the benefits brought about by globalisation. They often earn so little they cannot rise above the poverty line, and labour laws that should protect their welfare rights are routinely ignored.

Seeing the short film *The Story of Stuff*[2] encouraged me to question whether I, along with society at large, had been actively manipulated into buying more and more over recent history. The film suggests that consumerism as we know it was introduced after World War II as a strategy for reducing America's huge national debt. This period saw the idea of "built-in obsolescence" emerge, resulting in electrical and mechanical items that were designed to last only a few years, after which they would fail in a manner impossible to repair and would subsequently require replacement. President Eisenhower accepted this as a viable and legitimate way of increasing spending and creating jobs, the apparent engines of economic growth. This is the widely accepted "growth" paradigm that has taken root in our economy ever since. I question if it has now gone too far? Can our planet take it?

Reading further I was surprised to discover how marketing and mass consumerism came to be so entrenched in our current way of life. Edward Bernays, Sigmund Freud's nephew, who was considered the founder of public relations – the "Father of Spin" – was also responsible for organising the publication of his uncle's books and therefore the dissemination of his ideas in America. However, "While Freud tried to liberate his people from their subconscious drives and desires, Eddie (Bernays) sought to exploit these passions."[3] He used psychoanalytical ideas to market products including an infamous successful campaign to get women smoking in public. This misappropriation or interpretation of Freud's ideas had long-lasting and far-reaching effects. It seems business practices have encouraged the belief that desire is an innate human characteristic which can be manipulated to increase spending, by increasing the desire for an ever increasing range of products. Well it had certainly worked on me!

Changing my habits

I decided to take a look at my own behaviour as a consumer; I had to admit I got a real thrill when buying something new, a nice warm feeling of possession. Bargains were my speciality. But this wore off very quickly and pretty soon I would need another fix. Shopping was my drug.

I was left with an uneasy feeling that I was being manipulated day-in, day-out into being an obedient and profitable consumer. I began to suspect that my buying habits, while doing a great job of decreasing the Earth's resources, did little to increase the prosperity of the world's poorest. But more than this, I started to question whether I was living a life that lacked substance; where possessions were being used to fill a void that could never be filled on the material plane?

I had enough clothes and possessions to last years, so why did I still go looking for things to buy? Did I shop to bolster my self-esteem or was it that I needed to look my best in an attempt to please others? Could I learn to be more confident in my own skin, without forever trying to improve how I look?

In November 2008 I decided to experiment with my consumption of material goods. I wanted to be a responsible consumer but I needed to explore what that meant. Rather than mess around at the edges as I felt I had been doing, I decided to try something I had read about on the internet: "compacting".

Compacting

The Compacting movement originated in the USA in 2006, inspired by a group of San Franciscan friends who were dismayed by the USA's throwaway culture. In essence, it was a pledge not to buy anything new at all. The name comes from the word "compact", which means both to make smaller (as in rubbish compactor) and to make a pact (or promise). The group of friends decided to buy nothing new for a period of one year and provide mutual support to each other for this endeavour. It is now a community-led movement rallying against consumerist society and built-in obsolescence.

I resolved not to buy any new items (not just clothes) for a period of a year. The rules are clear: nothing new can be bought except those things listed in the table below.

You are, however, allowed to buy second-hand things from charity shops or similar and you can barter services for goods.

Unlimited	Limited
Food & drinks including animal and bird food	Hand-made local artisan gifts for friends & family
Toiletries (preferably organic or fair trade)	Gifts from charity shops
Cleaning materials (preferably organic or fair trade) – try to use refills or natural products	Original art work
Plants & flowers (preferably local or fair trade)	Plain underwear, utility socks and tights
Newspapers & stationery (recycled if possible)	
Medicines, spectacles etc	

To spice things up a bit, my husband joined me for the first year and we bet each other £100 that we wouldn't break the compact. In retrospect that was a mighty deterrent. For example when I saw a fabulous dress in Marks & Spencer's shop window at a bargain price of £15, it was very tempting to break the compact but as I would have lost the bet, it would have cost £115, which made it much less enticing.

How hard was it?
For me the important thing was to stay away from the shops. That did sometimes mean refusing invitations from friends and Saturdays were the most difficult because that had always been my regular shopping day. To start with I arranged special events like visiting a National Trust property or going for a long walk with the dog or even batch baking.

After a while I stopped missing the shopping trips and by Christmas I had begun to hate the crowds that appeared in the shopping centre. So I had to make do and mend. At one time I had no umbrella. The three I had at the start all broke eventually but it was uncanny that replacements appeared almost from nowhere: an acquaintance gave me one, a relation another, so it was only for a few days that I actually got wet. When I subsequently lost one of these umbrellas I felt mortified. Now that the things I had were potentially irreplaceable, they were becoming more important to me. I had to find it! Without a doubt I felt more dependent on others and wondered if having many possessions is a way of shielding ourselves from the need for support from others.

Our ten-year-old washing machine broke down last year and we were told it was beyond repair. I briefly considered breaking the compact and buying new, but was delighted to find the local repair company could provide a very similar but newer, re-conditioned item. I was greatly relieved not to have to traipse around the shops looking for a brand new replacement.

I really tried to buy as little as I needed. Originally I baulked at buying charity shop shoes, but I adapted to this, giving them a good clean and instead of thinking "yuk" I thought of how many shoeless people in the world would be happy to walk in mine. So I started to reflect more on the inequalities in the world, seeing my consumption against the larger picture. I was now beginning to consider my lot against the poorer of our society rather than the wealthy. It seemed good for my spirit to be happier with less.

It wasn't all plain sailing though, and I can't deny that on occasion I have seen someone of my age in a beautiful, fashionable outfit and the thought "I so want that" has flashed across my mind, but these days it is just as quickly followed by "but I don't need it". Once or twice I have caught myself feeling slightly shabby but on reflection that has given me a reality check and again made me appreciate how much I do have compared with so many.

Clothes remain important, I still like to look fashionable and I love dressing up, it's part of who I am and that's fine. However, I am now more aware of the role of fashion as a justification to consume and I go for timeless and lasting styles rather than high fashion. Charity shops are where it's at for me, and to be honest I still buy too much even from them; but rightly or wrongly, I've convinced myself it's all in a good cause as I do recycle it all back into the charity shop. If I need something special, there is a monthly sale of lightly used clothes in a local Church Hall, which has furnished me with some prized items.

I have had to be more inventive with presents for friends but have enjoyed filling second hand bowls and baskets with goodies. I find pretty plates in charity shops and create interesting presentations of soaps and toiletries. Local food, flowers and plants seem to be appreciated too. It's often the time to reflect on what a particular friend would really like that creates the best presents, not the money spent. It seems that previously I was spending more money just to save time. Perhaps this has led me to a more genuine approach to giving gifts, making material exchanges a real part of the relationship instead of just looking for something of appropriate monetary value.

So with the time saved from shopping what did I do? I used the garnered time for long leisurely walks in the countryside, marvelling at and meditating on the beauty all around me, free for all at no material cost. Or planting and weeding my garden, taking pleasure from my hands in the soil, watching and waiting for my plants to grow, taking pride in what was achieved. I have always felt earthed but until now, I hadn't seen what an important part of me this feeling of being connected to nature was. Now when surrounded by natural beauty I feel a deep sense of belonging to all that is around me, being part of something or of an energy that is so special that I can't even articulate it. It's as if I'm in the right place and in the right time and all is as it should be and I quite often feel a remarkable feeling of calm.

Moreover I see the need to come from deep gratitude for all we have. I have found that real gratitude somehow means needing less.

I actually see my past life as a shopaholic as being superficial. Recently I saw two young women, each carrying many designer shopping bags. I assumed they were shopaholics and found myself feeling sorry for them. Suddenly I realised how judgemental I was being and that this could have been me a few years ago. I felt both sad at my previous addiction and also glad that I now have different values. In some way it felt as if I had been avoiding my spiritual self, filling my time with meaningless activity, consumerism, and busyness for the sake of busyness.

Spreading the word
Compacting had such an effect on me that I wanted to spread the idea. I decided to give talks designed to get others to rethink their consumption habits. To the familiar three "R"s **Reduce, Reuse, Recycle** – I added **Rethink**: rethink your approach to consumption, rethink shopping as a leisure pursuit.

 Interestingly the questions were as important as the talk. I was able to explain more about the benefits that I had discovered from compacting and consider the reasons I had been addicted to shopping. I found it enlightening to hear myself answer openly, explaining how I used clothes and other new things as a way of bolstering my self-esteem. I hoped that this would help others to think about their own assumptions. From the feedback I received, I know this struck a chord with some of my audience. I also found sharing these insights rewarding. From the shopaholic at the beginning of my story I now found myself in a very different place and wanting to take my personal insights forward.

I am very concerned that our society and economy encourage younger and younger people into this trap of consumerism. You only need to look at fashion magazines to see the way they encourage dissatisfaction with ourselves by using enhanced body images. Even the most beautiful women in the world are not deemed acceptable enough to be left untouched. What does this say to our young people – and older ones like me for that matter?

My compacting talk led to a certain amount of media publicity which has helped me to become more active within the wider community. I have been amazed by the interest generated. I have even heard that my compacting message reached Hong Kong and Australia via the BBC radio network.

Future

Three years on and where do I now find myself? I still have too many things. I suspect I am a long way from being totally cured of my "affluenza" but I am happy to be in remission. I do try to use less of everything and not to waste anything. Some of my friends see the point but others don't and a couple have commented that we should all be buying more to help businesses recover.

I still have to avoid the sales, knowing my weakness for a bargain. Of course I've been tempted to buy new items and occasionally I've succumbed. I lost weight and bought a few items at the beginning of the year but on the whole, I'm still mainly on the wagon and consider very carefully if and when I need to buy new, including items for the home.

I now dislike shopping and feel rather dismayed that it continues to thrive as a leisure pursuit. Nothing worse than a convert is there? Although some may see my views as radical, I believe strongly that consumerism is really a substitute for authentic living. Does buying the latest gadget/car/clothes really make us happy? Or is it an avoidance strategy fuelled by a flawed understanding of what fulfils us and driven by advertising's manipulative machinations?

For myself, I have gained more time and understand that my connection to nature is what really makes me happy. Will I continue with my non-consumption? I have changed in a way that has surprised me, as well as my friends and family. I feel more in tune with my values and content with my lot. I also enjoy my ventures into advocacy. My overall aim is not to give up consuming altogether, but to be a considered consumer and I certainly feel I have a lot to consider as our beautiful planet appears to be reaching a time of crisis.

More than anything I also realise that I must be responsible for helping to preserve what we have. Perhaps through these changes in my behaviour I have found at last a spiritual purpose – to take this work forward in any way I can. I have found, coming from gratitude for nature in all its wondrous beauty and interconnectedness, that consumerism truly makes a poor substitute.

Having now seen the bigger picture, I can't help but be motivated by the words of Satish Kumar[4]:

> *So the solution is not just to replace fossil fuels with bio-fuel, but replace our quantitative consumerism with a qualitative lifestyle change. We need to move away from more and global to less and local, from accumulation to enjoyment, from employment to livelihood, and from desire to delight. Rather than consumption of natural resources, we need a culture of appreciation of the natural world.*

Notes to Chapter 5

1   Andrew Simms of the New Economics Foundation, New Scientist 2678, 10/08

2   *www.thestoryofstuff.com*

3   Tye, L, 1998. *The Father of Spin: Edward L. Bernays and the Birth of Public Relations*. New York: Henry Holt, p.197. Quoted in Shankar, A., Whittaker, J. & Fitchett, J., 2006. "Heaven Knows I'm Miserable Now." Marketing Theory, 6 (4), 485-505.

4   Kumar, S, 2002. *You Are Therefore I Am: a Declaration of Dependence*. Dartington: Green Books

6

I Don't Want to be a Passenger in Life
Johannes Moeller

On one of those rainy days, I watched the extended version of *Lord of the Rings* in one go. Twelve hours later I emerged again from the world of adventures, noble deeds, suffering and triumph, betrayal and friendship, and shining purpose that helped me endure sitting on a sofa for far too long. Afterwards, I felt drained to the bones. As I slowly regained my sense of reality, I thought my life would make so much more sense if I could just pick up a sword, gather my friends and pack my bags to fight for what I believed in, to fulfil a purposeful role in this world that I saw as much in danger as "The Shire".

My situation, however, seemed just a little bit more complex than that. I was about to leave university. My room was covered in journal articles and lecture notes. There were drawings and mind-maps on my wall brainstorming my options for the future. Boxes of campaign materials were stacked in the corner. My guitar served primarily as a dust collector and drying rack. Trying to predict my final exam questions seemed easier than anticipating what the right next step for me would be.

Three years at university had given me plenty of opportunity to accumulate knowledge about the state of the world. I understood the principles of climate change, ecological overshoot, globalisation, money as debt, and the psychology of human addiction and behaviour. My feeling of responsibility became stronger with my growing awareness and an increasing sense of privilege. Overwhelmingly, my sphere of responsibility seemed huge compared to my sphere of influence.

I was confronted with a twin challenge: I now needed to author my own life, and I wanted to find a way to co-author the world around me. How was I to make a living for a start? How could I live in a way that would not make things worse by emitting too much carbon, using too many resources, and abusing other people's labour to make my life easier? And then, how could I not only manage to be a polite passenger in life, but become an active part in shaping the story of our world positively?

In this chapter I weave together stories of how I navigated these questions, and how this has given rise to my work with young adults who also found themselves at a crossroads in their lives with the desire to shape the story of the Great Turning. I particularly want to share the challenges and insights that I came across co-creating and co-facilitating the Catalyst Course. Catalyst is a weeklong residential programme and network for young adults from diverse backgrounds who are making important decisions about their lives at this critical time in human history. It exists for people who want to make a positive difference in their own unique way while living purposeful, sustainable and fulfilling lives. Catalyst is part of Embercombe, a social enterprise and land-based education centre with the mission to "touch hearts, stimulate minds, and inspire committed action for a truly sustainable world".

During my last few weeks at university a painful reality was surfacing. I had studied psychology and started to learn first-hand about one of the most complex human phenomena: choice. "What are you going to do after university?" my friends and I asked each other on those rare occasions when we met up between preparing for exams. More often than not there was a heaviness and tiredness attached to this question. I had surrounded myself with people who were exploring how to live life differently. We campaigned against climate change, for renewable energy and fair trade, baked our own bread and grew some of our own food, attempted to change university policy, and educated ourselves and others about the social and environmental issues of our time. As we approached the end of our course, most of us were struggling to find a path by which we could continue living the belief that a different life and world was possible. I cringed when I heard some of my friends say, "Now we have to get into the real world." There was an intangible barrier between where we currently were and where we aspired to be after our course. The barrier was woven together by the reality of debt, self-doubts, the expectations from families and peers and realising that the world's problems are huge and one's own ability tiny in comparison. This was reinforced by cultural drivers such as restrictive definitions of success or fear of failure. To me it looked as if the energy of youth to create the new was choked by the worry about ever finding a job and the anxiety that comes with uncertainty about the future. It felt as if we were trying harder and harder to fit into a stream that was drying out.

When it came to the time I had to decide what to do next, the only sensible – and possible – decision to me was not to decide. Going for an option that existed did not seem to be what the world was truly asking for. I wanted to stop thinking about things, give myself space, to get my hands into the soil and hammer nails into wood. Allowing myself to find a way of doing this rather than "the sensible thing" is a decision that I'm proud of.

I'm grateful that the world around me, particularly my family, instilled in me the trust that I can create my own reality and that I do not have to cling to what exists to feel secure.

A few weeks later I found myself sitting in my new home, a little caravan in the woods. I loved to hear the raindrops on the tin roof before I went to sleep and to see the giant beech tree in front of my door each day I stepped out. I enjoyed every second of my five-minute walking commute to work. It took me through the forest and meadows, past the yurt village and compost loo. As a volunteer at Embercombe, I was busy working on the land, in the workshop and kitchen often till late at night, yet I felt I had space. My days often ended with inspiring conversations around a bonfire. The Embercombe staff gave me a sense of the energy and potential that is unleashed when people gather around a common purpose. The other volunteers were my peers in the exploration of other ways of living. And the groups of children, teenagers, corporate managers and others who attended courses stimulated discussions about what it means to create change in people, organisations and society. All this was deeply satisfying, sustainable and made a difference. It deepened my sense of how I wanted to live.

The idea of the Catalyst Course came from my own experience and witnessing so many other young adults struggle to make decisions about how to live and find ways of engaging with the big social and environmental issues of our time. What had benefited me was what I thought was needed: a non-judgmental space that allowed aspirations for another world to blossom, and enabled people to find their own way to live and contribute in this radically changing world. "How can we prepare for and shape an uncertain future?" became the question around which a community of young adults and the course was formed. Embercombe provided the fertile ground to make it happen and the model for what became Catalyst: a blend of working in the gardens, one-to-one coaching, facilitated group work, experiential challenges, storytelling, and time for reflection in nature, all set within the context of the pressing social, economic and environmental changes of our time. While the idea for Catalyst took shape, Kanada Elizabeth Gorla arrived at Embercombe. A long-time associate of Embercombe, and with a wealth of life and professional experience, Kanada brought a lot of the expertise to the vision of Catalyst. She had worked as an opera and theatre director and as a leadership development consultant for managers of multinational corporations and social enterprises. Her ability to liberate individuals and teams from limiting beliefs, fears and assumptions, and stimulate greater awareness, responsibility and choice, became core to what Catalyst became. Together with many others and the Embercombe staff we developed the model for the course.

Although the need for Catalyst was so obvious, the next two years felt like pushing a giant rock up the hill. I felt immensely passionate about it, but struggled to find the words to talk or write about it. I soon discovered that this was a common thread for most people who were drawn to Catalyst. For people building their path by walking, there is no map to show the way. There is no set language or phrases that describe what is unique, new and emergent. Many participants described how much they struggled to explain themselves to parents and friends. This struggle is an integral part of being true to what can be rather than to what has been. Later I realised that talking about Catalyst was difficult because there is no commonly accepted language for deep exploration of purpose, self and the wider world. Asking questions about making a living in changing times and how to contribute to a more sustainable world is unusual and often unwelcome. "What does it mean to you to be a human being at this particular time in human history?" is not a question that gets asked at a careers advice bureau.

But Catalyst did take off, doubling in number each year for the first three years. One of the main reasons for this success was the engagement of other people who I would call wayfinders or leaders, people with whom the programme resonated deeply and were willing to take the risk to run with it. There was Charlie Stephenson, the first person who booked onto the course, and who then recruited two more participants and paid for one friend to join him after I had told him on the phone that we might have to cancel it because of the lack of participants. There was Jacqueline Bagnal from Exeter Business School, who turned up at Embercombe after finding out about the course online, searching for opportunities she could offer to her students. She and her colleague Inmaculada Adarves-Yorno started to find funding for their students to join the course. Countless people helped in other ways. Writing this, I feel a rush of appreciation for everyone who played a part in putting the puzzle together, revealing a picture of what many envisioned.

Interestingly, it also took two years until I began to more fully understand what was most important about this work. It is about growing one's own inner freedom: the freedom of letting the what, how and why of life blossom from one's embodied feeling of aliveness rather than from pre-existing beliefs and assumptions. It is the freedom to stretch out of the comfort of what is known and courageously venture into the unknown. And it is the freedom that comes from fully accepting oneself as an individual, deeply connected to nature, other people and what is happening in the world. As the course unfolded I learned that without such inner freedom we would simply continue creating the same old patterns in the world and ourselves, and not create the emerging new; we would continue on the paths that were provided to us rather than searching for new ways.

This search for inner freedom, and the richness and challenges that go with it, come across in Minty's story. She participated in Catalyst a few years back, using her experience on the course to write her dissertation about how to facilitate conversations that stimulate change. Recently, Minty got in touch again, and wrote, "I'm on the uncertain, unmapped journey which you talk about in your writing." Inspired by Catalyst, Minty had decided after graduating from a top-ranked UK Business School not to continue with what the people around her expected, but to explore what she really wanted to do with her life. She did not want to be constrained by her strong feelings about what she "should" be doing or conforming to "the done thing". She wrote, "if no one was telling me what to do, or I didn't put any pressure on myself to do something because of judgment from someone else, what would I be doing?" This question led her to start working on an organic farm and volunteering at a community garden with disabled people. She reflected, "Through being curious and interested and simply being willing to have a go I've learned so much about working with the land, and how interconnected everything is – how important the soil is for the plants, and how everything can be reused and recycled for something else." Although she loved her experience, she also wrote, "Right now, I'm having a bit of a goalless, unmotivated, uncertain phase. I'm just going to be with that and am really working on not having too much judgment about it which is definitely challenging."

Feeling lost, unmotivated and confused at times when on a journey of exploration is a common theme for other young adults on similar journeys into uncertainty. I was moved to hear that Minty had "a goalless, unmotivated, uncertain phase", and allowed herself to be in her experience rather than judging and escaping those feelings by going back to how she lived before. It makes sense that such feelings arise when entering a space of uncertainty. Motivation in our society is so often contingent on the approval we get from doing what is expected of us. Yet, how can we transition into new ways of living if we cannot give up the goals that we and the world around us see as worth living for, and find the courage to embrace the uncertainty that waits beyond?

Ben was on the path of becoming a lawyer. Being aware of the vast inequalities and natural destruction in the world since being a teenager, he decided to devote his life to making a difference. Ben felt that the state of the world was his responsibility, and whatever small actions he was taking never felt enough. When he came to decide what to do with his life he thought that law was the best tool for fighting against the problems he saw. His decision to become a lawyer came as a shock to his family, who could not picture him in such a role because of his sensitive and creative nature. Just a few weeks after starting his studies he joined Catalyst, finally confident about the impact he could have in the world. He reflected, "Through the course of the week I was deeply confronted with myself and began to realize that the perception I had of my place in the world would never sustain me, and if I was to truly make a difference it must be though engaging in not only what I think is important but also what I love doing… I have always been deeply passionate about the arts, but saw only the individualistic ego that pervades most of mainstream theatre and art. After Catalyst I began to realise that this doesn't have to be the case. Theatre can be a weapon for liberation, and art a tool for social cohesion and environmental education. The artist has the capacity to imagine a better world and bring it into existence." Ben changed his course of study after Catalyst. Still at university, he has since started a company with other like-minded people, Cultivate, which works with school children in Brighton to co-create edible gardens and encourage experiential, creative environmental education. He has also been creating, devising and performing theatre plays as part of the "Funeral of Lost Species" projects with Feral Theatre. Ben risked following his passions rather than his preconceived ideas of how to have greatest effect in the world. He combined doing what he loves with what he believes is really important for the world.

Many other young adults I worked with were seeking to integrate the personal with the global. I found that this integration, or knowing how to contribute to this world in transition, was not always the main issue that young adults were struggling with. Much more frequently, giving oneself permission rather than holding oneself back and "having the courage to act upon what you know to be true" was the bottleneck. This courage is what Tim "Mac" Macartney, the founder of Embercombe, defines as the heart of authentic leadership.

"I'm not good enough to really do this", "I have to please others with my decisions", "I can't do this because otherwise I won't be accepted", "I need to be successful", "It is not OK to be really upset about this", "I have to do this perfectly and not do mistakes", "I have to be rational about this", "I need this relationship". Many participants told stories about their inner voices that repeated themselves internally, holding them back from moving into a direction they knew to be right.

When I first met Lucia on a Catalyst Course, I asked for her name. "I'm Lucia, or Lucy, whatever you want to call me." I asked, "Which name do you prefer?" "I really don't mind!" Slightly provocative, I said, "I want to call you by the name that you prefer. Which one is it?" "The one that you prefer," was the answer again. This dialogue continued until we decided to call her by the first name she had mentioned. Lucia was a highly intelligent, creative, sensitive and caring young woman. Through the week we spent together, I learned how she would never share her opinion when it would clash with others, that she would do anything for other people, and would never ask anything for herself. As she was passionate about environmental issues, this was a dilemma. What she valued and believed in jarred with the world around her, and consequently she would mostly shy away from expressing her values through words or actions. Her Catalyst Course experience was not about trying to fix this, or inquire into where this pattern came from in her life. For her the course was about entering a safe playground to experience what it is like to express herself fully and courageously. Her story was a great gift to many others on the course. Many felt that they held themselves back from bringing their passions, beliefs and values into the world.

Lucia's story was particularly influential to Richard, a strong and energetic young man from the north of England. Richard had been unemployed most of his time since he left school, and came to Embercombe and the Catalyst Course through a government scheme to support young adults to get into work. When he reflected on his own experience, he recognised that he was almost the opposite of Lucia. He did not really "do" emotions, and consequently was able to act without much emotional consideration. To no-one's surprise, he had run into trouble with people around him and the police a number of times. Imposing what he wanted onto the world was what felt comfortable to him. This had also cut him off from relating to other people and the world around him empathetically. Daring to step into relationship authentically was his challenge that he courageously stretched into during the course. Being in relationship opened up the possibility to fully participate in life and the world around him. In recent history, humans have shown how able we are to impose our will onto the world, literally changing the landscape of the planet. It seems enabling people to create change and express themselves through action in the world is only one side of the coin. The other is to learn how to create change in sensitive relationship with the self, others and the wider world.

When I ask Catalyst alumni about what supported them most since leaving the course, the answer often is the relationships, friendships and community formed on and since Catalyst. There is a simple power in spending a week together with diverse people who do not judge each other and who share a deep concern about what is happening in our world today; people who want to support each other to unfold their own unique gifts, passions and skills to lead a life that is deeply fulfilling and contributes to the unfolding story of our world. Ben, who changed his mind about becoming a lawyer said: "The ever-expanding community of Catalyst alumni shows to me that I no longer need to strive to be a complete jigsaw puzzle 'saving the world' on my own, but a single piece in a far greater story."

An un-named elder from the Hopi Nation in North America said about the times we live in, "The time of the lone wolf is over. Gather yourselves." I see Catalyst alumni and their extended communities going on courageous adventures together that make a difference, living together in purposeful ways and starting exciting projects or companies together. The land and community of Embercombe has become a home for alumni and many other people. It is a place for them to return to once in a while to rekindle their courage to author a new story of their own lives and the world around them.

In this company, I do not have the feeling that the energy of youth to create the new is choked by a fear of the future and by trying harder and harder to fit into a stream that is drying out. I do not get the sense that people simply choose an existing option that promises a straightforward pathway to success. Rather, I see people embracing uncertainty and developing their inner freedom to create new patterns in the world and themselves, ones that are in greater harmony with the people around them and nature. And I see young adults from diverse backgrounds making use of the immense privilege that all of this contains: the privilege that enables them to question the reality around them, that makes them hear their own inner call to live differently, that gives them the resources and confidence to translate this into action, and to find the friends with whom to enjoy the ride. Personally, I feel this loose, diverse and decentralised community of people enables me to keep exploring the question of how I can not only be a polite passenger in life, but become an active part in the unfolding story of our world.

7
A Journey to the Heart
Patrick Andrews

Wednesday morning. Winter. The house is dark and quiet. I go downstairs, light the fire, make a cup of tea, then do some gentle stretching and there's even time to dance, quietly, moving in time to tunes on my iPod. But this is soon interrupted as I hear Dasha and Lucas stir and then come downstairs, breaking into my peace.

So the day starts in earnest – feed the cats, feed the chickens, tidy the kitchen, make breakfast, take Lucas to school. I return home and it is time to work – hours hunched in front of a computer or on the phone. Later on, there's more cooking to be done, more chores.

Before I know it, it is evening time and I am trying to resist the temptation to flop in front of the TV, but am also not attracted by more computer time. Whatever I do, I rarely manage to relax, although I feel a deep need to.

Sometimes it feels like my life is an endless list of things to do, of responsibilities. I wouldn't mind except that I am not quite sure why I am doing it all. Intuitively I feel something is happening in the world – something big. I know there is a Great Turning happening, but what's my place in it? Maybe if I slow down, reflect on how I got here, and pay attention, some meaning will emerge.

In my early life, until I was 30, I suppose I had a fairly easy time. Without working too hard, things just came to me. Maybe I was loved very much – I felt a deep confidence in life and trusted that everything would work out fine.

I had a solid start, with kind, hard-working parents, a stable upbringing and a private school education. As I remember it, my parents were busy most of the time. My father was always at work (he was a partner in a firm of quantity surveyors), and my mum had to cope with looking after a big house and three active boys largely on her own. I learned to keep my head down and not be too demanding. "I want gets nothing!" was a common refrain in our house. So I would stick my head into a book, following the adventures of heroes such as the Famous Five, Frodo Baggins and, later on, James Bond.

When I was twelve my chance came to live my own adventures. My parents sent me and my two brothers (one older and one younger than me) to a summer camp deep in the Norfolk countryside. We spent the whole time in the fresh air, canoeing, hiking, playing ball games and sleeping in tents. In the evenings we sat round the campfire singing songs. I loved every minute. My brothers hated it. Next year I came again, on my own, for two weeks, and kept coming until I was sixteen. I think what I loved was the sense of freedom – we were supervised but not controlled, a contrast with what I experienced at home and at school. I also loved the closeness to nature. On my last trip, ten of us took off on a 90 mile, eight-day hike around Norfolk, pulling a cart filled with camping gear. Now we were certainly out of control, the two adults who were nominally leading us struggled to deal with this group of 15- and 16-year-olds, not quite sure whether to govern us or to join us. I tried drugs for the first time, one lad stole some milk, there was lots of sexual tension (and no doubt some sex, although I missed it!). For me it was an absolute eye-opener. The highlight was an overnight hike along the old Roman road, Peddar's Way, 33 miles long. Slipping past villages as the whole world slept, tasting carrots just picked from a farmer's field, kipping on the narrow wooden pews of an ancient Norman church for a few hours, I felt alive!

Back in the "real" world, I was following a conventional middle-class path towards a professional career. Without struggling too hard, I went to university and then qualified as a solicitor. Still, I didn't always follow the straight path. Immediately after qualifying I left my firm to go travelling. "What about your career?" a colleague asked me, incredulously. I didn't really understand the question – it felt like the right thing to do, and that was enough for me. The career would sort itself out when I got home. I got married, backpacked around southeast Asia with my new wife and then worked and travelled in Australia for a year before returning to the UK. Sure enough, soon after our return I charmed my way into an excellent job with a large company.

In those days I didn't think too much about my choices, even apparently major ones. My career in the law, for example, was really chosen for me by my school careers' master (he offered teaching as an alternative but my parents didn't think much of teachers). I didn't even put much thought into marriage – I simply went with the flow and it happened quite easily.

I'd met Alison at university, where she studied botany and geography. She was always heading off with her wellington boots for field trips in peat bogs while I was stuck in lecture theatres learning about jurisprudence and administrative law. It was clear from the start that she was keen on me – I wasn't so clear or so committed, and it took at least a couple of years before I knew I really loved her. Alison had an inner beauty and a deep love for and understanding of people that constantly surprised me. Whether she was stroking a dog, holding my hand, speaking to her family or identifying wild plants, she gave herself joyfully and wholeheartedly. She opened my heart in all sorts of ways.

And then she died…

I was 30 at the time and seemed to have everything I could want in life. I was working as a corporate lawyer for a large aerospace company based in Montreal, Canada. I loved my job. I was part of a great team and it felt like we were doing really important work, helping this company grow. I was happily married, enjoying life in this vibrant city. And Alison was pregnant.

At the end of the third month of the pregnancy, a very small lump, no larger than a pea, appeared just below Alison's ribs. It arrived without warning or fanfare. We weren't sure what to make of it and decided to get it checked out. From there, everything accelerated very quickly – I found myself in a dark and scary place, helpless to save myself as I was sucked down into the abyss.

It turned out the lump was a malignant tumour, on the liver, and it was growing fast, because of the pregnancy hormones. Three weeks after we first noticed it, the lump was as big as a melon. An emergency operation was planned, and shortly beforehand, a CT scan was done. The results came as a hammer blow. The scan showed the cancer was all over the body; in the lungs, the ovaries, the lymph glands. There was no point in having an operation, we were told, it would have to be chemotherapy. And that meant having an abortion. Alison would be dead within two weeks if she didn't have it, they said, because the tumour would keep growing. Besides, the baby wouldn't survive the chemotherapy.

We cried for a whole day. That night, Ali looked me in the eye, held my hand and said, "I want to kill myself." What could I say? She was absolutely serious. I took her in my arms and held her tight. Somehow we made it through the night. Maybe the lowest point of all was the abortion, two days later. It was hard to imagine anything Alison would have wanted less. Yet it felt like it was our choice, even though the doctors told us we had none. And we knew that almost certainly Alison would never have a chance to have children again.

How to describe the next eight months? Alison amazed everyone with her courage and grace, fighting her illness while getting on with her life. As for me, as long as she was around I could bear just about anything, and I focused on supporting her. After the abortion, the chemotherapy dramatically shrunk the tumour to almost nothing, and we had a few months of hope. But in time the cancer returned with a vengeance and before I knew it, I was standing by Alison's grave.

It felt as if the flow of life had stopped dead. I couldn't really cope, although I managed to put up a good pretence. Without Alison around, I couldn't even cry, not at least for several months after she had died. I just shut down, unable to express my emotions. What was going on inside? I don't know. It is all buried too deep. It has been a habit of mine, when under stress, to escape into my head rather than to acknowledge and deal with the emotions.

Gradually I re-built my life, or a pale imitation of a life. I went back to work. I couldn't engage with it in the same way but at least it gave me something to cling to amongst the wreckage.

Some healing did happen. I had counselling which helped me to get over the inevitable guilt feelings of still being alive. My vulnerability and fragility no doubt showed themselves, despite my attempts to put on a brave face, and I was helped by some good friends to express some of my pain.

By the time I went to Russia, two years after Ali's death, I was starting to get myself reasonably under control. Those emotions that hadn't been expressed were buried deep enough that they didn't disturb my day-to-day life. But they had provoked a restlessness, a deep questioning. I hadn't been able to settle in my old job in Montreal, which had given me so much satisfaction previously.

So I escaped – not for the last time. A fax came in from the general manager of our joint venture in St Petersburg, saying, "Help, I need a lawyer." I took the fax into my boss's office and said "I'll go!" My posting there lasted fifteen months. It changed my life.

I found St Petersburg a magical place. The city itself is beautiful but it was a special time too, just a few years after the break-up of the Soviet Union. Everything still felt new and raw, as the people got to grips with a market economy and re-building their social structures. The Russians I met were full of life, expressing their emotions with great warmth – quite the opposite of what I was used to and just what I needed. I started to feel alive again.

One day, after playing volleyball with colleagues, I slipped coming down some steps in the shower and banged my elbow. I ended up in the American medical centre and a doctor took me in to be treated by Dasha, a beautiful German physiotherapist. It was love at first sight.

I found Dasha quite mysterious – she wasn't like anyone I had ever met. There was a wildness about her, an untamed quality that was at once thrilling and slightly scary. She was brought up in a small, conservative wine-growing village near the Rhine, and had left to seek adventure. Although her dream of being a rock musician had been thwarted, she followed her heart and ended up in Russia, in a relationship with a rock star. When I met her, she had finished that relationship and was not in a hurry to start another one. She intended to leave Russia, as soon as she had sold her apartment. As it turned out, this didn't happen for another year.

In my clumsy way (I wasn't used to doing the chasing) I started courting Dasha. I invited her out to a concert first, and then we met up several times over the next weeks and I thought it was going very well. But then she mentioned in conversation that she was a "devotee" of an Indian holy man. I was horrified. "That's the end of that," I thought to myself. After all, I had been brought up as a Roman Catholic, which had been enough to convince me not to meddle with religion. Yet I wasn't entirely closed to exploring spirituality. I had unanswered questions from Alison's death. As I stood by her bedside, a few minutes after she had died, I had stared at her body and then looked around the hospital room wondering, "Where's she gone?" Her essence had departed, leaving an empty shell, mere flesh and bones.

In any event I was so smitten with Dasha that I was willing to suspend any scepticism. Nine months later we travelled to India together. After two months there, mainly spent in an ashram, we were married in a ceremony conducted by a Brahmin priest. It is amazing how in life the apparently impossible can, with time and patience, become the most natural thing in the world.

This marked a deep shift in me – I started to see the world through new eyes. Sai Baba, the holy man in the ashram we visited, offered the most profound, revolutionary yet simple of teachings. "Love all, serve all," was his main message – live your life in a spirit of service to others. He talked about five "human values"; love, peace, truth, non-violence and right conduct. In fact, I came to realise, he offered a modern day version of universal teachings by ancient masters such as the Buddha and Jesus. In his mouth, these dry dusty teachings came alive. It blew my mind.

By the late 1990s Dasha and I were back in the UK, and I was working for a large multinational retailer. It was a high-profile role, handling multi-million pound deals, working with Goldman Sachs and other investment bankers and taking plenty of foreign trips. I enjoyed it for a couple of years but my experiences in India had caused me to see everything in a new light, and I started questioning the whole ethos of the business.

I first had an inkling of the global ecological crisis, and western society's role in it, years before. Wondering about the causes of Alison's illness, my mind had latched onto food as a possible trigger. The more I learned about industrial processes for food production, the more appalled I became. I gave up eating meat, cut down on refined foods and started choosing organic products. Now I was starting to make new connections. It seemed clear that multinational companies were making a huge contribution to the ecological crisis, with their focus on growth and "wealth creation". The words of Vandana Shiva echoed in my head, "This so-called creation is based on destruction."

I remember travelling in a taxi in Shanghai, where I had gone to help establish a joint venture to build Western-style stores. We passed a row of small family-owned stores specialising in hardware, some selling paint, others wallpaper, or ladders and so on – what we call "mom and pop shops". It was colourful, diverse and lively. One of my colleagues observed, quite casually, "These are the sort of people we are going to put out of business." And a voice inside my head asked, "Why is that a good idea?" I realised that there was no way that I could ask that sort of question within my organisation – there simply wasn't a place for that discussion. Yet it went to the heart of our work.

This was a confusing time – at weekends I would read ecological magazines saying that big companies are ruining the world, and then on Monday morning I would go in to work and help a big company grow even bigger. I started surreptitiously looking around my office for the "evil empire". Was it the CEO? No, I was sure it wasn't him. The head of finance, perhaps? No, not her either – I didn't like her but I respected her. In fact all I could find was people like me, doing their best to make sense of life and their place in it. So why were they, we, collectively and systematically destroying the planet in pursuit of profit for distant shareholders? It made no sense.

I knew I had to get away, to get some perspective on this. Yet I was reluctant to just surrender my generous salary. Eventually an opportunity came up to take redundancy and I grabbed it with relief, vowing never to work for a big company or as a lawyer again.

So began the wandering stage of my career, which continued far longer than I ever imagined, and is only just drawing to a close, ten years after I left the corporate world. It has been a challenging time. I had no clear strategy – I just knew I had to try something and see what happened.

I took the first job offered to me. This was really meaningful and rewarding work, setting up and running a charity for the sailor Ellen MacArthur, taking children with cancer on sailing trips. Yet it wasn't what I wanted to do in the long term and after a year I moved on. I then got involved in fair trade, which I saw as an antidote to the unfair trade often practised by large corporations, spending a few months working for a food importer. I was surprised to find that overall it was no better than other businesses I had worked for. On the positive side the staff were highly motivated, working with passion for their shared values. Yet I felt there was too much tolerance for abstract discussions that distracted from the day-to-day running of the business. The main problem was the board, made up of volunteers who didn't really know what was going on in the business. This didn't hold them back from trying to set strategy, aimed at achieving their lofty ambitions to change the world. I am all for lofty ambitions but they need to be grounded.

My next venture, after my contract with the fair trade company came to an end, was aimed at revolutionising the management consultancy profession. I did this with two friends and we had a lot of fun but, like my previous roles, it didn't last. It really seemed I was lost.

The problem was that I was off script. Previously I had always known where I was headed in life, following the path laid down for me from a young age.

I feel I was trained to conform, firstly at home, then at school, and then in my corporate roles. Now I had to create a script of my own and live it, something new and scary. I remember forcing myself to do an illegal act, riding my bicycle through Regent's Park, simply to experience breaking the rules.

During all this time, Dasha was quietly supportive but she couldn't help wondering what was happening to her corporate lawyer husband. I wasn't exactly clear myself. On the positive side I was learning a lot. I read widely, from Zen Buddhism to radical economic publications, and was very taken by writers including EF Schumacher, Dee Hock and Ricardo Semler who presented alternative visions of organising based on the same human values I had heard about in the ashram. It made sense that the combination of new communication technology and a rising ecological awareness would result in brand new ways of organising that we have only just begun to imagine. Could developing these new ways of organising be my mission in life? I felt it could.

On the negative side, I seemed to have fallen off the career ladder and had no plan about how to get on it again. And then Dasha became pregnant, at a time when our finances were at a low ebb. So to rebuild the family finances I took a crazy job, working for a UK property developer, doing deals in Russia and commuting to Moscow twice a month. This felt a bit like sleeping with the enemy ("Welcome to the dark side!" a lawyer friend of mine said gleefully). Property development, along with investment banking, is capitalism at its most unashamed. But in fact the work came as rather a relief from the lonely slog of self-employment and I couldn't help admiring the entrepreneurialism of my colleagues, wandering about the new "Wild East" finding deals.

Yet in time I realised that such work comes at a cost. "You are an absentee father," said Dasha, to my surprise and horror. None of my colleagues had what I would consider a healthy family life. They were young and single, or middle-aged and either divorced or settled into a notional marriage where their main interaction with the family was to send a cheque home once a month. This wasn't for me. Two years into the job, I started to negotiate my way out. But where would I go next? The answer turned out to be simple – Riversimple.

A few years previously I had started working with Hugo Spowers, an Old Etonian with a radical vision for the car industry. He was developing a highly energy-efficient, hydrogen-powered car with a revolutionary business model – the cars would be leased, not sold. The part that really got me hooked was that he was keen to re-think the legal structure of the business.

We both felt there are better ways of inspiring people than to ask them to serve shareholders and shareholder value. We wanted to set up a business where the board would be accountable to a mixture of "custodians" representing various stakeholder groups, including the planet. As I was winding up my work in Russia, an opportunity came to join Riversimple, the newly formed car company, full-time. The role was to create a brand new ownership and governance structure. Finally I had a sense of doing work that was using my skills and had meaning.

In the meantime our home life had been transformed by the arrival of our son. I cried when Lucas was born, feeling joy and also a sense of release after finally realising this cherished dream. When Lucas was one year old we moved out of London to the countryside, near the south coast of England. Falling into the middle-class trap, we bought a large house with a large garden. It would have been fine if I continued to earn a generous salary. But that wasn't to be counted on, as my rollercoaster ride wasn't over. As a start-up, Riversimple had limited funds and we struggled to raise more. Within eighteen months I was receiving a reduced wage and not long after there was no money to pay me at all.

The last two years have been a crunch period. Having limited savings, almost no income and a large house to maintain, I couldn't at first admit the truth about our financial situation to myself or Dasha. I suppose I felt uncomfortable doing so – as a man, I ought to be able to bring home the bacon, and clearly I wasn't doing so.

So I withdrew into myself, much to the concern of my family. In their different ways they tried to get through to me, but to no avail. I simply wasn't ready to listen. Instead I just kept plugging away at my mission, trying valiantly but ineffectively to make sense of the role of organisations and businesses in the world.

So where am I today? On the surface, at least, nothing has changed much. There is still a lot of uncertainty in my life. Yet in recent weeks I have understood something, helped in part by writing this story, which has changed everything.

Firstly, I have realised that my mission is endless and probably fruitless. I don't think it is possible to make sense of what is going on in our society today, not with logic anyway. How can you stay sane when one minute you are reading a report about the oceans dying, in part because of overfishing, and the next minute your loving wife offers you a tuna sandwich? How can you reconcile the joy of a family trip to the beach with the knowledge that you went by car and therefore contributed to carbon emissions? You simply can't, I have concluded, and you shouldn't even try.

You see, I have made the mistake of trying to solve the "problem" of modern life using my head. Yet relying too much on our heads is what got us into this mess in the first place. The head is good at analysing things, chopping them up and dissecting them, but poor at understanding relationships between things. And it is our relationships that need sorting out if we are to make it through the Great Turning in any sort of shape. It is the heart that now needs to take the lead.

My heart reassures me: "You don't need to understand anything," it whispers. "All is well. Just be."

In my youth I relied on and trusted my heart much more. But after Alison died I closed down the connection to my heart, as a way of numbing the pain. I need to re-establish that connection, if I want to heal my own pain and that of others. Which means I have to slow down. The heart, you see, speaks to me in whispers. If I rush about, trying to do too much, I simply can't hear it. When I do hear it, it helps me to connect up the apparently random, chaotic nature of the world into patterns, to make sense of it all.

The significance of this goes further. I realise that what is true at an individual level is true at an institutional and societal level too. Our rushing-about society provides no space for the quiet voices to be heard – the downtrodden, the feminine, the future generations, our Mother Earth. We have no hope unless we can learn to slow down and listen.

This, then, is my work in the Great Turning. It is not to "save the world" (after all there is always more world to save). It is not to transform the world of big corporations. It is simply to lead with my heart, wherever I go. This is what will allow me to re-connect with my own self, with my family, my community, the planet and life itself. There is nothing else to do…

8
The Truth Mandala
Clare Power

The haunting call of a pair of black cockatoos draws me to the door. They usually signal a change in the weather but for now the early morning air is crisp and invigorating. As I look out I see drifts of mist still lingering in the valley below, and I can hear the faint tinkling of bellbirds. I drink in the scene, taking sustenance for the day ahead.

It's good to stop for a moment. I've been inside the local community hall for a couple of hours preparing for today's workshop and haven't had to time to pause and reflect on the day ahead. I am offering a workshop developed by Joanna Macy called the Work that Reconnects. This is an experiential workshop where we use a range of different activities, rituals and discussions to face the challenges of living in a world in crisis. The workshop is based on the idea that it is empowering to share the pain we feel for the world openly with others rather than suppressing or denying it.

Although I have facilitated this workshop a number of times I feel a bit nervous and, in a way, surprised to find myself here. In 2008 I was very fortunate to attend a ten-day intensive retreat with Joanna, her husband Fran and 28 other people from around the world in the redwood forests south of San Francisco. It slowly dawned on me while I was there that not only were we benefitting ourselves from attending the retreat, but we were being encouraged to take this work back to our homes to share with others.

I had particularly loved the way that Joanna integrated rituals into the retreat. Rituals and sacred ceremonies have been a core practice for humanity since our earliest times. They have been used to connect us to ourselves, our communities, our environment and our cosmos. When I participate in a ritual I feel as if a deep yearning within me is being met. I think that's because, to me, this is a way of creating a safe space for deepening into experiences beyond the norms of daily discussion or dialogue. The clear boundaries of an opening and closing, the agreement of respectful communication between participants and the different forms of creative expression provide a sense of freedom. In Joanna's deft and wise hands at the retreat, our rituals were profound and moving experiences. I feel excited and privileged to be able to share them with people in the workshops that I offer, and at the same time, I feel a great weight of responsibility that I provide a safe and supportive environment within which participants can experience the power of the rituals.

My favourite ritual in the Work that Reconnects is called the Truth Mandala, and yet this is the one I feel most nervous about facilitating. This thought reminds me that I need to make sure that I am fully prepared before people arrive, so I leave the doorway and return to the hall.

In just over an hour, 18 people will arrive to participate in the workshop. Cushions and chairs form a circle in the centre of the room and I've decorated a table with an exuberance of autumn leaves. We will begin the day with what is called an "acknowledgement of country", where we pay respect to the traditional indigenous custodians of this land and remember the elders past and present.

The day is then divided into four sessions based around the themes of gratitude, honouring our pain for the world, new ways of seeing and going forth. The first session helps people to get to know and begin to trust each other so that they feel they can express themselves fully. We begin with people introducing themselves by explaining how the object they have brought with them, such as a flower, a photo or a small sculpture symbolises their connection with the Earth. Then through a few different activities, we explore the concept of gratitude which helps us to recognise our interdependence with all of life and the creatures, plants, ecosystems and people involved in all aspects of our existence.

At morning tea I am reassured by the chatter among the group as people start to feel more at ease with each other. This is important because we've come to the second session of the workshop called "honouring our pain for the world". The Truth Mandala is the mainstay of this session and often the most confronting part of the day for participants. The Truth Mandala is the name for a ritual that is designed to break down the social barriers that prevent us from talking about how we feel about the state of the planet and other things that concern us deeply. It provides the opportunity to speak openly about how it feels to be living during this time when there is so much ecological destruction, injustice and suffering in the world. Because the Truth Mandala enables people to move beyond their usual comfort zone, and because this sort of expression isn't common practice in our society, it can take a while for the group to settle into the process.

I remind myself of this as I look around the group of men and women, ranging in age from their early twenties to their seventies, seated in a tightly formed circle. I find this ritual both exhilarating and personally challenging to facilitate. I notice that my body is tense and my hands are clenched. My mouth is dry and as I reach for my water bottle, I wonder why I put myself in this situation time and again when I have pangs of anxiety about my capacity to do justice to the Work that Reconnects. Breathe and trust, I tell myself. This is not about you. You are just a conduit for this work; this ritual has been performed hundreds of times around the world.

Before beginning the Truth Mandala I guide the group through a practice called "breathing through". This is a breath meditation that we can use to be present with the feelings that come up for us during the Truth Mandala and in any situation in life where we experience feelings of pain. I explain: "This is a really useful practice to use at any time that you are aware of suffering and have the impulse to throw up defences against it. Using your breath, you can choose not to separate or defend yourself but instead to feel the pain, breathe it in and through your heart. The important thing is that you don't have to hold on to it, you can breathe it out again through your exhalation. This enables you to be with your feelings but not to get stuck in them. Joanna describes this act of dropping our defences as radical because in contradiction to our usual responses of closing down or denying what we are seeing or feeling, we can connect more fully with it. Joanna has a lovely saying: if we feel a great ache in our chest as if our heart could break, we need to remember that our heart is not an object that can break, and if it were, it is said the heart that breaks open can hold an entire universe."

I rise and walk into the centre of the circle, setting a bag containing symbolic objects on the floor. "Imagine this space is divided into four quadrants," I say as I trace imaginary lines across the circle. I squat and take a short solid stick from the bag and place it in one of the quadrants. "This stick represents our anger; the anger that we may feel, the fury and the outrage that it has come to this, that such injustice and pain is being inflicted in our world." I pour a small heap of dry leaves on the floor in the second quadrant. "These leaves represent our sadness and our grief for the losses that are happening in our lives and in our world; the landscapes, the cultures, the languages, the beings, our hope." I feel the cool solidity of a large granite stone that I draw from the bag. "This stone stands for our fear, the fear that is different for each one of us, but it's the fear for what's happening in our lives and our world. This is how our heart feels when we are afraid: tight, contracted, hard; in this quadrant we speak our fear." The fourth object is a wooden bowl. "This bowl represents our sense of emptiness, our sense of being overwhelmed, our powerlessness, our confusion and our not knowing; our hunger for what is missing." I then place a cushion in the centre of the circle. "You might have something to share that does not necessarily fit in any of the quadrants, so this is where you might like to express it or something else such as a poem, a prayer, a song or a movement."

Returning to my place in the circle I explain, "You are invited to enter the Truth Mandala and express your feelings with the help of the objects. And it's OK if you want to enter the circle and not say anything, and it's also fine if you don't want to enter at all. People generally find that it's a powerful experience just to be present in the circle. If you do enter the circle you can move between the objects, and if you decide during the ritual you need to come in again, that's fine.

"And there is an important guideline which is that the Truth Mandala is not a place for dialogue, or a soapbox or an opportunity to admonish or persuade others of your point of view. It's a place to speak from your heart and know that you will be heard with respect. When someone enters the Truth Mandala and speaks we listen in silence and as they return to the circle we say, 'We hear you, we are with you.'"

I'm never quite sure when to talk about the flip side of the emotions symbolised by the objects. I've seen some people do it at the beginning of the ritual and others at the end. I struggle with the part of me that wants to immediately reassure people of the positive sides of the feelings they are being invited to express. Here we are poised at a moment of great uncertainty about what will occur in the ritual and I am aware of the trust that everyone has placed in me as the facilitator of the process. Looking around at the group, I trust my sense that now is the best time.

"So," I say, "you may ask, 'where is hope?' Well, hope is the very ground of this Mandala. To speak our truth does not deny hope, it can enrich and strengthen it." I move to each symbol holding them up in turn and say, "It is also important to recognise what underlies the emotions represented by these objects. For example, when anger is being expressed what you are hearing is a great passion for justice. When you hear sorrow know that what is being expressed is love, for we mourn what we love. When you are hearing fear, know that fear is evidence of our capacity for courage and the emptiness that's expressed creates the space that is needed to allow the new to arise."

I quickly scan my notes to make sure I haven't forgotten to say anything important. I seem to have covered it all and ask if there are any questions or comments. Everyone shakes their head, so we are ready to begin.

As a way of expressing our intent I dedicate the ritual to the welfare and healing of all beings and our world. We open the ritual with a short sounding chant to focus our attention in the present.

As the chant subsides a wave of anxiety passes through me. This ritual raises strong emotions. What if someone flips out or cries interminably, or perhaps says something that others find offensive or confronting… "What ifs" crowd my mind.

The heavy silence feels as if it could either smother or liberate possibilities. I know that someone will enter the Mandala eventually, and once one person takes that step then others will follow. However it feels like it's taking a long time for anyone to move. Perhaps I should enter the circle first.

I notice some shuffling to my left and am relieved that Marg moves in and sits by the stick. She raises it to her chest. There is a long pause before she speaks and when she does her voice quivers. "I have three young children," she says, "and I don't know what the future holds for them. It's never been so uncertain." She flails one arm in the air and her voice becomes stronger. "I do as much as I can. I write letters to the paper, I grow veggies and I have rainwater tanks and solar panels on my roof. I'm always agitating for change at the school and we've started a garden and a climate change group. I'm involved in so many different things that I'm not even there for my children half the time." She grips the stick firmly with both hands and her voice is infused with anger. "And do all these things make a difference? How can I look my children in the eye and tell them that we'll be leaving the world a better place for them. I feel such rage. Can't we see we are jeopardising our children's future, their birthright?" She returns the stick to the floor and reaches for the bowl, cradling it in her lap. "What do I do?" She looks around the group. "What am I meant to do?"

It's hard when someone asks a question of the group like that. Our impulse is to answer, to help, but the ritual is about listening and accepting, not discussing and debating. I see people nodding their heads acknowledging Marg's question and her pain. "I just keep going,'" she says in answer to her question. "I don't give up, I show my kids that we don't give up." She puts the bowl down and moves slowly back to her place.

I lead the group in saying, "We hear you, we are with you."

Both Sascha and Michael start to move at the same time. Michael beckons to Sascha who enters the circle and sits by the leaves. Her head is bowed as she runs them through her fingers. She looks up. "I've decided not to have children," she states and I see looks of consternation pass over some faces. "I'm twenty six, and I want children but I can't bring a child into this world." She sniffs and I see a wash of tears on her cheeks. She barely whispers, "It hurts. I ache." She clutches her belly and bends her head to the floor. I notice the tissues being passed around the circle as she moves back to her place.

"We hear you, we are with you," we intone.

A moment later Michael crawls into the circle, and kneels on the cushion. "I nearly didn't come today," he says, his voice shaking. "I've given up. I can't bear to say it, but it's true." He looks at the objects and takes the stone. "I've run out of hope for us to get our shit together in time. So what do I do now? Hunker down and work on my farm and live from day to day? But where do I get the hope to plant the seeds for the next crop? And what's the use now? I'm an organic farmer and my neighbours are planting GM crops." He grabs the stick and squeezes it with both hands. "And that's just me; look at what's happening to farmers all over our country, all over the world. Forced off their land, or seeing it poisoned and their crops mutating. I never thought I'd say this, I've lost hope." His body heaves as he sobs. I feel my chest tighten, and a panicked sensation sweeps through me. Michael is a stalwart of activism in our community, where is hope if he has none? I remember the breathing through meditation, allow myself to feel that panic and then to breathe it out. I need to do this a few times before I feel that I can just hear Michael without my reactions affecting me so much. Gradually his sobs lessen in intensity and he sits still and silent. He exhales loudly several times and raising his head looks around the circle, smiling gently. "There I've said it. And the funny thing is, you're right, there is hope here in this circle. I feel like one of my fields after the rain. Thank you."

"We hear you, we are with you."

The air in the room feels dense. I wonder how people are going with this process. "Remember to practice breathing through," I say, and notice a few people taking deep breaths. Freya enters the circle. She is a bright chatty young woman and I'm surprised when she says, "I haven't been feeling anything. I've shut down, I'm disconnected. I work, I play, I party. I don't know what I feel." She reaches for the bowl. "I've cut off from my feelings because it's all too big. I don't know what to do. I'm only young but here I am, with all of you." She laughs and says apologetically, "Sorry no offence intended. But where are the people who are my age and why they aren't caring?" She waves her hands tentatively over the objects and then clasps the stick. "Why do I have to take responsibility for a world that others have fucked up?" She places the stone in the bowl and pours a handful of leaves over it. "I don't dare feel my sadness. It's too huge. Maybe I'd never stop crying." She sits for a moment stirring the leaves in the bowl before putting the objects back.

"We hear you. We are with you."

Sonya reaches into the circle and takes the cushion and hugs it to her chest. Isn't she going to enter the circle? Does it matter; do I need to say anything? I had said be creative with the process after all. She then moves slightly into the centre and draws all the objects close to her. She places the stone on the cushion saying, "I take this stone and speak of my fear for all the species that are becoming extinct." Sprinkling some leaves over the stone she says, "I scatter these leaves for my sorrow that we don't care enough to stop it." She places the bowl upside down on the stone. "Enough of being paralysed and inhibited by fear, I am no longer ruled by it." Taking the stick she stands up and says, "I claim my right to speak out for the voiceless. I refuse to be silenced any longer." She tosses her head and smiles at the group. "You'll be hearing me roar!"

"Yes!" I hear someone respond, and a few people chuckle.

"We hear you, we are with you."

Matt stands and walks purposefully into the circle where he reaches for the stick. "You know," he begins, "I'm Mr articulate activist out there saving the world. Mr busy with no time to stop and feel, even if I knew how to. I didn't get the title of this workshop before. But now, I can see for me it's not just reconnecting with all of life, it's also about reconnecting with who I am and why I'm doing all this stuff." He slowly turns on the spot looking at each person momentarily. "I'm in awe of your courage," he says, "maybe some day I can talk about my feelings in the same way."

"We hear you, we are with you."

Sylvia enters the circle. She curls up on the cushion and sweeps each of the objects close to her belly. Then she moans; a deep bellowing that seems to be coming from the earth itself. Occasionally she murmurs some words, "the oceans, the forests, greed, starvation, violence, hope taken from innocent children". The tissues circulate around the room and sniffles punctuate the silent spaces. I feel engulfed by sadness and once again reach for my breath to allow the feelings to let them move through me. Sylvia stays in the circle for a few minutes. She becomes so still that I wonder if she will move. What will I do if she doesn't move, how long should I wait? I look around the circle. Some people are staring intently at the floor, and others looking compassionately at Sylvia. This hasn't happened before, and I just need to sit with it and see what happens. I'm relieved when she slowly rises and placing her hands in a gesture of prayer bows to the group.

"We hear you, we are with you."

One by one each person enters the circle. Tanya doesn't speak at all. She takes each object in turn, closing her eyes for a moment as she holds them and then returns to her place. Martin talks about the difficulty of being a man who tries to talk openly about his feelings and how this causes him to be ostracised and labelled as crazy. Jake, an older man, weeps as he expresses his fears of time running out; his time and time for humanity. Arly speaks of her anger about uranium mining and the proliferation of nuclear power despite what happened in Fukushima. Milos fills the bowl with leaves and mourns the utter incomprehensible stupidity of humans for causing Earth's sixth great extinction.

The gaps between people entering the circle begin to lengthen. I sense that the Truth Mandala has almost run its course and ask if anyone else would like to enter the circle.

Paolo has not yet spoken. He moves into the centre and holds the stick above his head. "I want to shout, to yell, to run outside and knock on all the doors, to stop the cars, burst into shopping centres. Why do we have to share our fears in private like this? Why can't people hear the scientists? We have so little time. I could rattle off so many statistics about the acidification of the oceans that will have such devastating effects on the food chain. Or the unthinkable consequences of four degrees of warming on billions of people. Can't people hear this? A devastated food chain, that means starvation. Billions of people. That's us. We always seem to think it's other people." He drops the stick and stands up, turning as he looks around at us all. "I feel like it's driving me mad. Why can't we see what we are doing? I know the raves about why, the psychological reasons and all of that. But for God's sake, the alarms bells are clanging and telling us that our very lives, our children, every ecosystem and culture are under the greatest threat. Why can't we change?" He heaves a great sigh and presses his hands into his temples.

It feels like the group has taken a collective inhalation and frozen. I breath out loudly and in again. It takes a moment before I can lead the response.

"We hear you, we are with you."

Several more people return to the centre before there is a long pause and it seems that everyone who wishes to has had their turn. It's time to close the ritual and I draw again on Joanna's words saying, "The Truth Mandala has now ended. Let us honour the truths that have been spoken. Truth-telling is like oxygen, it enlivens us. Without it we grow confused and numb. It is also a homecoming, bringing us back to powerful connections and our own authority."

We stand and I nod to Jude who is leading us in a dance. I learnt this dance recently and thought its joyful clapping, finger clicking and foot stomping would be a fitting way to leave the Truth Mandala. I look around the circle and see people laughing and smiling as they place their hands on each other's shoulders in the first steps of the dance. I feel grateful and honoured to be with such a group of people who have just bared their souls to each other, and communally plumbed their grief.

After lunch we come to the third session: "New ways of seeing". Before moving into this session we discuss the experience of the Truth Mandala and how by facing the dark we can also see the light, and that the two are not opposites, but co-exist. We talk about how the Truth Mandala can help us to feel our sense of interconnectedness with each other and with all of life. Sonya points out that this is a shift in thinking from the dominant worldview of separation and polarities to a worldview where we see that we are part of the web of life.

I sense that people are quite tired by the final session of the workshop, which is about what we will take forward into our lives. As a gentle activity, I pass around chunks of clay and invite everyone to create a representation of something they will do in the next month in response to the workshop. When each person speaks about their clay piece they also share their reflections on the day. Moira observes how soft and clear everyone's face seems. I can see what she means as I look around the group, and I also notice the ripening friendships forming between people. Sylvia expresses appreciation to the group for their openness and courage in sharing their innermost selves so generously. Sascha says that she has spoken aloud things in the group that she has never uttered before and that this has somehow given her a renewal of hope. Jake thanks the young people present for being brave enough to confront the mess that his generation has made for them and apologises that they even need to be in this situation.

We are lingering and the warmth between the group is palpable. I am about to close the workshop when Marg sums up the mood. "I wasn't sure about coming today and whether I was up to participating in this. But I'm so glad that I came. Thank you everybody. I came in wearing lead boots and now I'm leaving on tiptoes."

When I arrive home I make a cup of tea and sit outside on my deck. The change in the weather heralded by the black cockatoos this morning is moving in and a cool southerly wind stirs the taller trees in my garden. I feel a deep exhaustion and realise how much tension I held before running the workshop. I try to quell the voice that is reminding me of things I didn't say or do, or berating me for the way I explained a process. Instead I focus on people's comments as they were leaving, at the gratitude they expressed for having an opportunity to share so deeply with others, and the renewed sense of hope and energy that they were carrying home with them.

What an honour it is to be able to give people the opportunity to participate in such a day. Images from the Truth Mandala cross my mind and I think about how paradoxically nourishing it is to actually be able to express those feelings we are taught to suppress. The wind is strengthening now, tossing leaves and small sticks into the air. I move out into the garden and breathing in I inhale deep gratitude to Joanna and all her collaborators in creating this work, and I breathe out my thanks to be carried along the wind out into the world.

Note: This story is a fictionalised account of a Truth Mandala. I have drawn on my experiences of participating in and facilitating a number of Truth Mandalas to create this story.

Great Turning Artful Inquiry
James Aldridge, Chris Seeley & Kathy Skerritt

In parallel to the writing of the *Stories of the Great Turning,* curators James Aldridge, Chris Seeley and Kathy Skerritt invited other visual practitioners around the world to respond to Joanna Macy's five guidelines. The Great Turning Artful Inquiry is an unfolding, mutually-constructed process with ongoing dialogue between artists though a Facebook group called the *Great Turning Artful Inquiry.* At the time of writing the group has 84 participants and is open to new members.

Here, eleven artists' work is shown, each with an excerpt from the writing that accompanied each piece. Many of the works – spanning events, dance, objects, sculpture, websites, film and visual art – are oriented more towards process than final product.

We hope you are inspired to make your own artful responses to the Great Turning through these images and words.

Cathy Fitzgerald

the neighbours (2012) HD 00:34 cathy fitzgerald

This work is part of an ongoing (since 2008) slow art and ecology forest transformation project; it is a still from a series of short experimental video works that are making up the *Hollywood Diaries* (the wood, in Ireland, is called Hollywood).

Like a growing forest this is a long-term process with no fixed end date. In the last year I have begun to focus deeply on experimental cinema for my own practice development and, via my PhD website *www.ecoartfilm.com*, begun to create an online resource for the very small field of cinema theory and practice that seeks to better attend to the natural world.

Nika Newcomb Quirk

In this Artful Inquiry, for a long time I did nothing but sit with Joanna's personal guidelines. Then, the Dark chose me to express our relationship. I had many ideas about inviting others to work on this with me, but the busy river of life washed them away. I brought my journal to a shady porch for an after-lunch reflection and restoration time. I swung back and forth, back and forth on the rustic, cane-seated rocker, listening to bird calls and the singsong of distant conversation. I let myself step back a foot inside myself. I looked in fascination at the spiraling within the bank of vines crawling up the porch railing in front of me. Then, I noticed the dialogue of broken hearts rising up in my consciousness and I drew *Forgiveness, Shared*.

Liesel Beukes

I can still taste the sea in my tears was inspired by a piece in Joanna Macy's amazing poem, *The Bestiary,* that she wrote on endangered species:

> *Dive me deep, brother whale, in this time we have left.*
> *Deep in our mother ocean where I once swam, gilled, and finned.*
> *The salt from those early seas still runs in my tears.*

To "Come from gratitude" starts with remembering our interconnection, which is a big theme in my work. Once we have remembered that we are connected, compassion for other beings and the Earth will become a natural response. We can then join hands in serving the Earth and its beings.

Claire-Lilith Suscens

I am "Daring to vision" myself as an artist at this Earth-time, working with ritual, movement theatre and as a poet. In my journey through ecological communities, I have started to focus on poetry composition, sourcing from movement improvisation practice a creative expression of my own process with and through the myth of separation, towards an embodied sense of the fact of my interconnectedness.

This image is a still from my first experiment with the idea of *Ritual, Co-creative Improvised Performance* – a twenty-movement improvisation piece in a ninety-minute show I produced called *Interconnectedness*, in the Universal Hall, Findhorn, April 2010.

Debbie Warrener

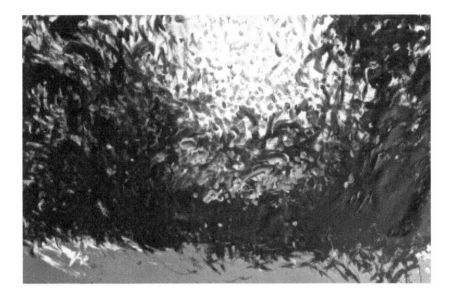

This work I have called *Despair Tunnel*. Recently I have been connected with quite a lot of despair – a feeling of a great abyss opening up which can be quite scary. What I know is that once I stop fighting, being afraid and trying to run from the dark or trying to get someone else or something else to numb or fix it – it does transform. This piece is connected with this sense.

I was interested to see that this piece the other way up almost looks somewhat Christ-like or May goddess-like – it is May as I am writing this. This for me seems to symbolise the light in the darkness once we stop and "see" the dark for what it is and turn it upside down. The dark and despair make a whirling dank fog of FEAR. Light and life are always there too.

Sophie Jane Twiss

In making *Earth Lady Breathing*, I was not so much illustating a scene or experience but my feeling, my response to the earth. The tree and womb are central, the tree of growth in heart space, the womb of love and creation, roots to earth and sky, connectedness. The figure is of devotion, of gratitude. Our transition to environmental conciousness involves listening to and honouring the voice of the Earth. I feel sorrow and darkness, beauty and love, gratitude and wonder at the Earth. I was mindful of these things when I was creating.

Merry Crowson

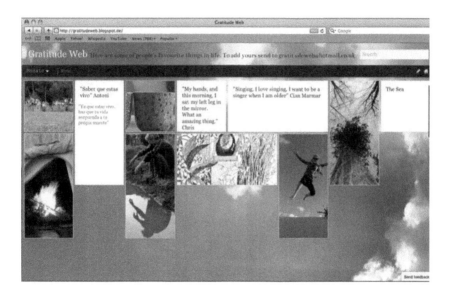

I am new to Joanna Macy's work so started from the beginning: Gratitude. As soon as I remember what an extraordinary experience life is – that we are able to see, hear, taste and touch the world – I feel a need to share. I know what I am grateful for, but what about my little cousin? Did I ever tell my best friend how glad I am I met her? Is my work colleague also glad to be alive? What does my sister think is the best thing in the world? I decided to set up a blog as a kaleidoscope of peak experiences and gratitude for life. I feel the process created a small pause to dwell on gratitude and take that energy into our lives. Feel free to take a peak and add your voice to the chorus. *http://gratitudeweb.blogspot.co.uk/*

Siobhan Soraghan

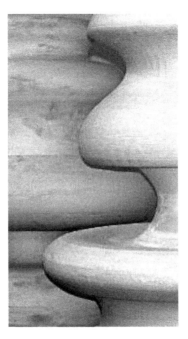

Adam and Eve are abstract sculpture pieces relating to "Don't be afraid of the dark". The dark unknown other "out there" can be a reflection of what we least like or know about ourselves. Here, there is both resonance and contrast, generating a beautiful balance. Each of these two plaster pieces was formed on a rotating spindle and shaped by a blade with the same curve – one piece was made using the positive side of the blade and the other from the negative side of the blade's curve. They belong to, and yet are autonomous from, one another. One felt more masculine, the other has a more feminine feel which I have acknowledged in their names.

Ruth Ben-Tovim

A Little Patch of Ground is an inter-generational food growing and performance project produced by Encounter Arts and inspired by Joanna Macy's the Work that Reconnects. I created this project in 2009 with fellow artist Anne-Marie Culhane coming from our shared desire to respond creatively to the challenges of climate change as well as to develop ways for people to come together across age, culture and social backgrounds to explore new way of seeing, being and doing together.
www.encounter-arts.org.uk

Jo Crowson

I made my *Great Turning Power Bag* with the intention to create an object that could remind me of gratitude on a daily basis. Every part of the bag holds meaning for me. I see so many different initiatives around me that together add up to a huge force for change, such as the possibility of creating a transition movement here in rural Andalusia and, of course, the spiritual activism I am exploring as I link my shamanic work with permaculture. And that brings me back to gratitude. My bag sings to my subconscious mind, reminding me what my real work is…

Karen Dodd

Motherly Eye specifically embodies gratitude for life and compassion in the space of the dark. The watchful guardianship and nurturing eye of the mother is depicted in a continuum with the rising up of fledgling life. This reaching for life mirrors the energetic force of all organic beings and perhaps even the (inorganic) beginning of the cosmos itself. Dynamic circularity in a spiral form also evokes the myth of the phoenix rising from the ashes, the new out of the old, a renewal of our planet, despite the darkness and despair.

9
Leaping Aboard:
Onshore Volunteer Work with Sea Shepherd
Elizabeth Claire Alberts

Six months into a scholarship-funded PhD programme in creative writing and my first academic teaching position, I wanted to scribble a letter of resignation to my university, pack a toothbrush and a few sets of clothes into a duffel bag, and leap onto Sea Shepherd Conservation Society's *MV Bob Barker*. When I first suggested the idea to my husband, Brad, he thought I was crazy. I couldn't just *quit* my PhD and volunteer on this ship, he told me. Hadn't I spent years working to get the academic position I had today? Didn't I just tell him last week how much I enjoyed what I was doing? And he was right. I did enjoy my PhD and teaching work. And I felt proud that I had earned a scholarship that paid me to spend every day researching young adult verse novels, a literary genre that had fascinated me for years, and to write a verse novel as well. We owned a four-bedroom house in the northern suburbs of Sydney. We were in the middle of redeveloping our property so we could subdivide. We had a mortgage, stacks of unpaid bills, and two ginger cats who fretted if either of us left the house for more than a few hours.

But I had just read a book that made me want to change everything.

The book, Peter Heller's *The Whale Warriors*[1], had actually sat unread on my bookshelf for nearly two years. When I eventually picked it up, my fingers curled crinkles into the pages as I read fact after fact that startled me awake. Heller narrates his experience on Sea Shepherd's *MV Farley Mowat* as the ship ventures into the Southern Ocean to protect the whales from the Japanese, who set out to kill hundreds under the guise of "scientific research". Between Heller's descriptions of fast-action ship ramming and vegan food cooking in the galley, he explains why protecting the oceans is so important. Yes, whales are amazing creatures, and it is easy for most people to want to protect them. But the entire marine eco-system is in serious trouble. More than half of the coral reefs around the world have already disappeared. Fish stocks are collapsing beyond repair. Hundreds of oxygen-dead zones have developed from all the noxious chemicals humans dump into the oceans. As Paul Watson, the founder of Sea Shepherd, says in Heller's book, the oceans are dying.

Of course I'd heard about these environmental problems before, but I had never recognised the severity of these issues until now. Why weren't more people talking about this? Why was Sea Shepherd the only organization that had ships in the ocean enforcing environmental law?

After I ranted and raved for weeks about wanting to drop everything and volunteer on one of the Sea Shepherd ships, Brad finally borrowed my creased and dog-eared copy of *The Whale Warriors*. My husband, in comparison to me, is not what you would call a "book reader". He doesn't often pick up a book on his own, and when he does start a book, he reads about three-quarters of it before casting it aside. Brad finished *The Whale Warriors* within a week. Soon, we were snuggled on our living room couch watching every season of *Whale Wars*, Animal Planet's TV series that documents Sea Shepherd's annual Antarctic whale defence campaigns. We yelled and cried with the crewmembers as we witnessed the Japanese harpoon a minke whale. We wriggled in our seats as we watched the Sea Shepherd ships roar across white-capped waters to intercept the *Nisshin Maru*, the Japanese factory ship. We leaned towards the TV as we listened to the crewmembers speak, recognising the same passion in ourselves that we saw in them. What we realised – more than anything – was the absolute cruelty of whaling, and the urgency to do something about it right now.

The more I learned about Sea Shepherd, the more I learned that we couldn't drop everything and jump onto one of the ships. When I emailed the assistant crew manager, he mentioned that it took four years for him to be called to action after submitting an application. Everyone, it seemed, wanted to volunteer on the ships. This didn't surprise me considering the popularity of *Whale Wars* and the quasi-celebrity status of many of the crewmembers. But as I trawled the Sea Shepherd website, I learned about a different way to get involved – onshore volunteering – that we could start right away. I emailed the Sea Shepherd Australia office asking for more information, and the Australian Coordinator sent me an application form and a manual detailing in dry prose how to run an effective fundraising and outreach stall. The photographs inside the manual – which looked like they were over twenty years old – showed volunteers selling Sea Shepherd caps and t-shirts behind banner-covered trestle tables. Onshore work didn't seem as glamorous as crewing on the ship, and at first glance, it didn't even seem as effective. But the ships needed money to stay in action, and onshore volunteering could help raise that money, right?

I filled in my application. Brad filled out his shortly after. I marched to the nearest post box and pushed the envelope into the metal slot.

A few weeks later, Brad and I got our first onshore "call to action" to volunteer at a film event at Fox Studios in Sydney. Paul Watson was flying to Sydney to speak at the world premiere of *At the Edge of the World*[2], a film that chronicled Sea Shepherd's 2005 whale defence campaign. I remember slipping into my black Sea Shepherd Jolly-Roger t-shirt and black jeans long before we had to leave the house. Brad also got ready early, shaving his face clean and ironing his black pants. We were the first ones to arrive at the cinema. Then, closer to the start time, more volunteers began to spill into the lobby. I spun around, shaking hands, collecting names, exchanging stories. I felt a rush of excitement as I listened to the reasons why others had decided to volunteer for Sea Shepherd. Many – like me and Brad – had read something about Sea Shepherd, or watched a film, or listened to Paul Watson speak at another event. And now they were here, two hands ready to work.

When the three coordinators of the Sydney chapter arrived, all the volunteers hurried to unload the trestle tables, the plastic drawers packed with merchandise, and other supplies from the truck parked outside. Once everything was inside the cinema lobby, we worked with the others to set up the merchandise and ticket tables. One of the coordinators called a meeting, running through the night's schedule. Brad and I raised our hands to help out at the ticket table. The doors opened. People streamed in and lined up for tickets. I checked off names and counted money. My heart leapt as I watched the ticket sales climb high into the hundreds and sprawl into the thousands. With every dollar I collected, I felt like I was saving a dorsal fin, then a fluke, then a blowhole, until an entire whale swam free and alive. Then I saved another whale, and another, and another. My feet ached and my stomach growled. I didn't stop for a minute. Brad also didn't stop. He engaged with every guest who came up to the ticket table, sometimes sharing facts like how 50-80% of the world's oxygen comes from phytoplankton in the ocean, or how livestock producers are responsible for over 52% of the world's greenhouse gases, which contributes to ocean acidification. When the ticket table was less busy, Brad shook one of the donation tins through the crowd, conjuring cash.

Later, when Paul Watson arrived, Brad and I slipped into the back of the cinema to listen to him speak. Reading about Paul and the issues facing our oceans is one thing. Hearing Paul speak about these issues is another. Every time Paul shared another earth-rattling fact, I felt the same fiery desire to drop everything and leap onto one of the ships. But I didn't need to leap onto one of the ships now. I was actually doing something now.

Brad and I stayed until the very end, working with the rest of the volunteers to pack the supplies back into the truck. We huddled together as the coordinators told everyone about the other events we could get involved with. There were market stalls, music festivals, educational outreach opportunities. Brad and I – as well as the other volunteers – said *yes, yes, yes.* We would help out. We would. The whole car-ride home, I couldn't stop talking about how good it felt to actually do something. And we could fit this kind of volunteer work into our busy lives. When I woke up the next morning, I headed straight for my study and wrote ten pages of my verse novel. We were busy, yes, but we could still do something.

The next event – a market stall at a music festival – was cancelled because not enough volunteers had signed up. Brad and I had put our names down, but the coordinators explained that one of them needed to be there, and none of the three coordinators could attend that event. Not long after, Brad and I started getting phone calls. Could we pick up the merchandise? Could we keep the merchandise at our house? Could we run the next event on our own? Did we want to take over the roles of the Sydney Coordinators?

The week those calls came, excavators and compactors roared up and down our steep hilltop property as Brad worked with our neighbour to prepare the site for the new shared driveway. Brad toiled from dawn until dusk, only coming into the house to drain a glass of juice or devour a sandwich. When I tried to talk to him about the coordinator roles, he shook his head. "I love Sea Shepherd," he said, "but I just don't have the time. We don't have time. We'll help out as much as we can, but we can't coordinate the chapter."

I knew Brad was right. But I couldn't stop thinking about the facts I read in Heller's book: whales being hunted to extinction, fish stocks collapsing, coral reefs dying. And I couldn't stop thinking how amazing it felt to help out at that film night. Although Brad wanted us to only commit to tabling at markets and other small events, I started taking on bits of administration work for Sea Shepherd. I counted the money after events and delivered it to the bank. I entered the after-event paperwork into the online databases. I phoned event organisers to confirm Sea Shepherd's attendance.

"You're taking on far too much, possum," Brad would tell me, sticking his head into my study to find Sea Shepherd paperwork scattered across my desk. "You've got your PhD."

"I know," I told him. "I know." But I was reading about the threatened blue-fin tuna now, and how Sea Shepherd fought to save the fish from extinction. I learned about Sea Shepherd's fight against shark finning. And so I filled out an order for new merchandise and conducted a stock-take. I organised the stationery box with new membership forms. I got access to the Sea Shepherd email account, and spent hours every day writing responses to volunteers, supporters, and sponsors. Before I knew it, I was actually coordinating the Sydney Chapter. Brad helped when he could, but I was largely doing it on my own.

Admittedly, I found the balance between my PhD and Sea Shepherd increasingly difficult. It wasn't just that Sea Shepherd ate into my time. I also found it hard to leave the exciting world of environmental activism. Since reading Heller's book, I had continued my research on the oceans, surfing the net for scientific articles, watching films like *Sharkwater*[3] and *The Cove*[4], and reading books like Charles Clover's *The End of the Line*[5] and Alanna Mitchell's *Seasick*[6]. The more I learned about the urgent problems facing the oceans, the more I questioned the importance of my doctoral work on verse novels. I particularly questioned my thesis component. Although I loved verse novels, and had spent years reading as many as I could and swooning at the emotion-packed free verse that typified the genre, I found it hard to justify the hours I spent reading arcane literary theory that seemed so removed from the rest of the world.

The creative writing component, on the other hand, I didn't question so much. Or, perhaps I should say, I didn't question my reasons for wanting to write. I knew writing was the right path for me by the way my mind constantly swirled with stories, and by the way I penned through paper notebooks faster than I could buy them. But I did start to question what I was writing. My verse novel was about a teenage girl who wanted to be a poet, but lived in a futuristic world in which no one read or wrote anymore. I still felt interested in this fictional world I had created, but when I opened my notebook to write, I stared at the white of the page and saw corals bleaching. I wrote a rush of words, then stopped, thinking of the chemicals that streamed into the ocean and leached out the oxygen. I considered changing my topic to something more environmentally themed, but I was well over a year into my PhD now and I hated thinking about all the time I would have wasted.

So I persevered. Even with all my doubts, I managed to get a large amount of research done and chunks of my verse novel written. Was it my best work? I'm not sure. But I got it done. I wanted to prove to myself – and to Brad – that I could coordinate the Sydney Chapter and keep up with my PhD. Still, I couldn't ignore the hunger I felt to learn more – and do more – for the oceans. I couldn't ignore the itch I felt to write beyond the world of my verse novel. Something was shifting in me.

Then I got an email from the Sea Shepherd Australia office, informing me that Paul Watson would come back to Sydney in November before leaving for the 2010/2011 Antarctic whale-defence campaign, "Operation No Compromise", and that a large fundraising event needed to be planned. I had become used to doing a lot of work for Sea Shepherd, but this email made me want to hyperventilate into a paper bag. The office wanted me to organise a venue, an MC, guest speakers, a VIP guest-list, AV equipment, food and drink donations, an alcohol license, auction items…the list went on and on.

This time, Brad laid down the law. He told me that I absolutely, most-definitely, without-a-doubt *could not* take on the task of organising this event on my own. He reminded me of all the time I spent on Sea Shepherd already. He reminded me that I was getting paid by my university to work on my PhD full-time, and that I had a responsibility to my university, to myself, and to him, to get on with my thesis and verse novel. He told me stories of people he knew who had organised events like this, and how it became a full-time job and took over their lives.

I hated recognising the reason in Brad's words, but I knew he was right. And so I did what I had never done the entire time I'd been involved with Sea Shepherd: I picked up the phone, called the Australian Director, and said no, I couldn't organise the event.

I thought I'd feel relieved after making that phone call. But instead my stomach knotted and turned. I hated hearing the disappointment in the Australian Director's voice, how he'd said "no worries" and quickly hung up the phone. I paced the house, asking Brad again and again if I had made the right decision. Of course he said I had. But I couldn't stop thinking about who *would* organise the event if I didn't. The former coordinators had already said they didn't have the time. And although the Sydney Chapter contained many dedicated volunteers, I couldn't imagine any of them having the time to take on the work of this event. I couldn't stop thinking about the oxygen dead-zones in the ocean, the depleted fish stocks and the dying coral reefs. I couldn't stop thinking about the whales and the sharks and the blue-fin tuna – and everything that Sea Shepherd fought to protect.

That night in bed, I sat up in the dark and turned on the lamp. Brad blinked as I told him that I had changed my mind, that I would call the Australian Director in the morning to tell him that I'd help organise the event after all.

"Possum…" Brad started.

"Please," I said. "Don't talk me out of it. I've made up my mind."

I knew what I was saying was crazy. I knew that taking on this event just didn't "make sense". But I also knew that if I didn't do this, it would be like slamming the door on this rush of passion that had burst so suddenly – and so voraciously – into my life. I couldn't justify the practical reasons for my decision, but I knew I needed to do this.

And so I dived head-first into what became one of the craziest – but also one of the most rewarding – periods of my life. I started waking up before the sun, tumbling into my desk chair with half-open eyes to work on my verse novel and thesis. Then, after lunch, I'd hurry to complete the regular Sea Shepherd chapter duties before I turned my attention to the fundraising event.

Thankfully, I wasn't lumped with all the work myself. The Australian Director enlisted the help of Lisa Rossi, a Sea Shepherd volunteer from Perth. Together, Lisa and I spent hours writing emails to potential venues, guest speakers, musicians, and businesses, asking for support and sponsorship. Many initial responses we received were "no", and I remember feeling quite discouraged. But then Lisa and I got our first big "yes" from the Bondi Pavilion in Bondi Beach, the most famous beachside suburb in Sydney. They said they could provide Sea Shepherd with the "High Tide Room" at a very minimal cost. Somehow this "yes" seemed to kick-start the event preparation and the wave of positive energy that followed.

Now that I knew the event would take place in Bondi Beach, I started writing a new round of emails. This time, I targeted businesses in the Bondi area. I tried to convey the importance of Sea Shepherd's mission. I pitched the unique marketing opportunity for them to get involved with a local event. Perhaps I was now using the right combination of words, because support began to pour in. Nearly every day, another email popped into my inbox telling me yes they'd donate some paintings for our auction, yes they'd donate surfing lessons, yes they'd donate some yoga class vouchers. And so many of these sponsors wanted to know: what else could they do, what else, what else? These emails fuelled me with hope. By seeing how passionate other people could become about Sea Shepherd, it reminded me how important this cause was. These emails blasted away any doubts I felt about spending too much time organising the event. They pushed me on, urging me to do more and more.

I organised a meeting with the other Sydney volunteers, sharing the developing plans for our event, which I had named "Bondi No Compromise". I loved watching the enthusiasm I felt spread through the rest of the volunteers. Everyone offered to do something. One of the volunteers commissioned his sister in France to create paintings for the event and to post them over for our auction. Another volunteer phoned me with the news that she had found a security company that would donate their services for free. One volunteer in particular – Veronica Makiv – threw an incredible amount of energy and resources into this event. She organised countless big-ticket auction items, thousands of dollars of wine and beer, musicians, an auctioneer, event banners, and high-quality poster printing.

Even though Brad had initially said he couldn't help out to a great extent, I noticed that he started making jobs for himself, contacting businesses about donating auction items and organising the vegan catering. When I said I needed to go to Bondi to pick up donations or post event flyers, Brad grabbed the car keys and drove me himself.

The weeks ticked by. I scribbled poems and read articles for my PhD. I sent sponsor logos to Sea Shepherd's graphic designer. I finalised the event schedule. I signed contracts. My mind became a blur of emails, phone calls, poems, sponsors, volunteers, guest-lists, thesis chapters, whales, run-sheets, speeches.

And then, the big day arrived. Brad and I rolled out of bed and sped down to the Bondi Pavilion to help set up. My mobile phone constantly rang. I criss-crossed the venue a million times an hour, working with the other volunteers to make sure everything was set up properly and that everything ran to plan. Hours melted away like minutes.

But these fast-pace, to-do list details are not what I remember most about the event. What I remember most are the moments when time slowed down: the heart-pounding delight I felt when so many people packed into the High Tide Room that we ran out of tickets; the peals of applause that shook the room after Paul's speech. Brad leaping onto the stage to hold up the surfboard for the live auction. The lit-up faces, the handshakes, the kind words, the cheques and fifty-dollar notes pressed into our donation tins as the public pledged their support to help stop whaling. I remember cheering with the other volunteers when we counted the cash, and announced that we had made $36,000 in pure profit to support the upcoming whale defence campaign.

However, what I remember most of all is the feeling that washed over me when I slipped outside into the cool night air and stood at the stage door to listen to the end of Paul's speech. I had been running around the venue all night, but for a few short minutes I forgot about the run-sheet on my clipboard, the notes scrawled on my hand, the thing I needed to do next. I took a deep breath and let the sound of Paul's voice wander through my mind. And this feeling of calm and happiness came over me. My thoughts regarding Sea Shepherd were almost always tangled up with questions and anxieties and tensions about time and commitment and whether I should be working on my PhD or Sea Shepherd. But in that moment, I didn't think of any of that. I just felt good about what I had done. I felt really good.

Brad and I stayed in Bondi that night, and instead of rushing back home the next morning to work like we usually did after a Sea Shepherd event, we took off our shoes and strolled along the wet sand on Bondi Beach. Our sentences meshed together as we repeated every detail of the previous night, over and over. I told Brad how good it felt to work with a team of volunteers and pull off such a successful night. I felt like I could do anything now. If I helped raise such a huge amount of money for Sea Shepherd, I knew I could do more good. And even though I sometimes felt doubtful about my PhD, I knew I could finish that, too.

"Have you ever thought," Brad said, "about writing about something different? Writing about environmental issues?"

"Yes," I said, feeling my heart pick up pace. "Yes, I have."

Brad grabbed my hand as we continued to wander along the beach. We watched children splash into the water, collecting sand and shells in plastic buckets. Surfers sprinted past us, dashing through the shallows to catch the waves further out. My mind raced into the ocean, too, diving into the froth, searching for stories.

Author's Note: "Operation No Compromise", Sea Shepherd's seventh whale defence campaign, was the most successful operation to date, saving the lives of over 900 whales. Although many believed this would mark the end of whaling in the Southern Ocean, the Japanese fleet returned the next year, and Sea Shepherd's work has continued. For more information on Sea Shepherd, visit www.seashepherd.org.

Notes to Chapter 9

1   Heller, P, 2008. *The Whale Warriors: On board a pirate ship in the battle to save the world's largest mammals.* Sydney: HarperCollins

2   *At the Edge of the World.* Dir. Dan Stone. Eagle Entertainment, 2010

3   *Sharkwater.* Dir. Rob Stewart. Warner Brothers, 2006

4   *The Cove.* Dir. Louie Psihoyos. Lionsgate, 2009

5   Clover, C, 2006. *The End of the Line: How overfishing is changing the world and what we eat.* Berkeley: University of California Press

6   Mitchell, A, 2009. *Seasick: Ocean change and the extinction of life on Earth.* Chicago: University of Chicago Press

10
Water Power
Gil Chambers

Sometimes I think I imagined that we built a hydro scheme. A fantasy, a memory of fiction, a dream I've always had since long ago, the romantic dream of self-sufficiency. But as I gaze out from the top of the orchard and look down over the roofs of our old farm home, down into the valley, green and tree-covered, then up the steep fields on the other side, up to the snow-clad ridge of Llangynidr mountain I realise that dreams can come true. The winter sun is low over the ridge. I feel its warmth on my face as I marvel, as I do every day, at how we came to be here, here, here in our place of paradise. It is the gurgling, rushing sound of water streaming down to my left, the soft continuous whining purr coming from the timber-clad building to my back that confirms that we did do it. We did install a hydroelectric scheme. The sounds are that of energy created by the power of water. The sounds of water under great pressure creating the soft purr from behind me as it is forced into a narrow jet to turn a turbine which drives a generator which creates the magic of electricity...

I remember the start, over five years ago now, the six words that Pip uttered that set us on the thrilling course of installing a micro hydroelectric scheme.

"We could install a hydro scheme," says Pip.

"I don't think we have enough water," say I.

"I could get our hydro engineer to come look," says Dai.

Dai is from Green Earth Energy and was visiting our home to discuss the installation of solar panels. The discussion results in our realising that we didn't need copious quantities of hot water. We do not have central heating and the hot water is heated by the stove, and most importantly we didn't have a south-facing roof.

A few days later a battered VW arrives in the yard and a young man emerges.

"Hi I'm Richard, Dai sent me to check for a hydro scheme."

"Great," we both say. "But I don't think we have enough water," I say.

We explained where it was so off he went to check. Most people go back along the track then up the path. Richard took off like a gazelle straight up the steep fields behind us. We went in and put the kettle on.

Perhaps I should explain at this point. The property that we, and by we I mean my partner Pip and I, bought in 1993 was a derelict farm about 210 metres up the south-facing slope of Tor-y-Foel mountain, the first of many lesser mountains leading up to the peaks of the Brecon Beacons. Our farm, Cae'r Hendre, translates as "Field of the Winter Home". For us, how we found it and bought it is another story; it translates as "the place dreams become reality". The farm comprises a 16th century Welsh longhouse with attached animal barn, large freestanding barn and other assorted outbuildings built around a large yard. A very lovely group of rough stone buildings built into the hillside. The attached barn is now Pip's studio, my drawing office and joint library. The barn and outbuildings opposite are now a holiday cottage and workshop. The big barn is waiting attention.

A short while later Richard comes galumphing down the field to announce, "Loads of water up there, make a great scheme." Then a pause. "Well, not a huge amount of water but what you do have is height, about 170 metres of height, this produces great pressure, sixteen bar of pressure."

"Sixteen Bar?"

"Yes that's over 230 PSI, take the skin off your hand. It'll work, it's the pressure of the water that will make it work."

So began our adventure into the uncertain edge of current technology, the world of generating electricity from the power of very little water.

Richard went off to design and cost the scheme. The technology was in its infancy so not only would Richard, as an engineer, design the scheme; he would also be making the "TURGO" turbine, stainless steel mounting and all the other bits and pieces.

Then we sat down to discuss the finer details. First we didn't own any of the land that the intake and pipe would be installed on, nor did we have any money to install it. The land above us all the way up to our spring is tenanted farmland so our first port of call was Dave and Myfanwy Evans, the farming tenants. They were happy for us to install the pipe across their fields as long as the landowner, Lorraine Lewis, was. We met with Lorraine who was excited by the idea and was keen for us to do it, so keen in fact that her husband Mike volunteered to help with the installation. This offer was a little scary as Mike was a retired military man.

We now had clearance on access to the land so now how to fund? What we did was borrow some money, ask neighbours and friends to physically help, apply for government and National Park grants – at that time government grants were available – sell Pip's artwork and most importantly do as much of the work ourselves.

The two major expenses in installing a hydro scheme are all the technical and manufactured bits – the intakes and forebay tank, the turbine, the generator, the high-pressure penstock pipe, the control unit and other electrical pieces; and the graft. In our case the latter would involve the purchasing, positioning and burying of 650 metres of 100 millimetre-diameter pipe down the mountain; constructing the intake boxes; building the brick structure for the turbine and generator, and the building that housed it; and trenching the 75 metres of power cable down through the orchard to the house consumer unit. There was little we could do about the manufacturing but we could do virtually all of the graft.

An abstraction licence from the Environment Agency was required before we could begin or receive the grant. In order to apply for an abstraction licence planning permission was required. We were told that we probably didn't require planning permission but would, nonetheless, have to apply for full planning in order to be told we didn't require it! As with every aspect of our installation fortune smiled on us. With amazing support from the Countryside Section of the National Park, a letter was sent stating that we didn't require planning approval. So, with paperwork in order, we applied for the abstraction licence. I must point out that dealing with the Environment Agency is not easy but with Pip's perseverance we were granted a licence.

We were now in a position to apply for the government grant. At the time the grant was £1000 per kilowatt-hour (kWh) generated. For us this would mean a grant of £3,300 for which you could apply online or on paper, but the former was given preferential treatment. As it turned out we couldn't apply online unless we had an accredited installer. The technology was too young, and as a result there were no accredited installers. We applied four times, each time being rejected. Each time the month's allocation of funds had been taken up by online applicants installing photovoltaics or B&Q wind turbines. Finally this scheme was withdrawn and a new grant scheme set up with no limits on the funds but with a maximum grant of £2,500. As a result we found ourselves £800 short of the funds from our original calculations.

Nonetheless, with great support from the staff at the National Park Countryside Section, we were able to secure a further 15% funding grant from their Sustainable Development Fund. We organised a sale of Pip's work that also included home preserves for sale and with amazing support raised a further 35% of the required financing. Some people who couldn't make it actually sent in donations.

Finally we arranged a loan from the local Credit Union which was keen to be involved, and thus we found the remaining funds necessary to start on the project.

Ian Evans, son of our farming neighbours, agreed to dig the trench with his beautifully restored mini-digger for a very low rate. He also helped us to retrieve the redundant domestic storage tank from the woods above us and brought it into the yard for us to clean. This was to become the forebay tank; that is, a water holding tank positioned just below the intake. When the tank was finally cleaned a bronze outlet was fitted with a gasket made from the cut-out sides of an old pair of Wellington boots.

Throughout we had the support of our neighbours and friends. I cannot stress enough how wonderful it felt to receive such generosity. Having made the decision to embark on this venture everybody seemed to gather round to help as though the enterprise was unstoppable once begun.

Richard had given us a list of all the materials required so we could order them direct, thus reducing the cost by not having an installer mark-up on price. So it was that in early June 2008 we were ready to order the materials and hopefully install. Unfortunately 2008 was also one of the wettest summers on record; it was the summer of the floods in Ludlow, Tewksbury and many other places. Ian, our digger driver was unable to get on the land until late August. The steeply sloping site was dangerous enough when dry; when wet it is potentially lethal.

We had begun to wonder where the 650 metres of pipe had got to when we received a call from Kevin Davies, who farmed the land at the top of the hill where the pipes were to be delivered. The lane up to his farm was too narrow for the delivery lorry so he had got the driver to drop the pipes off at their other farmstead nearby. "Great," I said, "give me a shout when you need a hand to bring them up." He never called, so after ten days I phoned again. "Already done it," he informed me, "took them one at a time on the front loader of the tractor each time I came back from the farm." I was speechless. With support such as this, how could we possibly fail?

We finally had all seven coils of pipe piled up on a piece of flattish land near the farm. The pipes were unravelled with help from Mike Lewis and our friend Mary Bennet. Then with much more help they were moved a distance of over a kilometre along the mountainside to the intake site.

An electric armour cable was to be installed alongside the penstock (pipe) to be used as a switch line from the tank to the turbine. Ian arrived with his digger having previously carried up the forebay tank by tractor. The first task was to dig out a base for the tank, and when this was done a metre-deep trench was begun leading along an old track before plunging down the hillside.

While Ian was digging Pip and I fitted the intake screens and dug trenches to take the pipes that would feed the forebay tank. When that was done we moved down to the house to start on the turbine mounting.

Dai Evans lent us his quad bike for moving materials up to the top of the orchard via his adjoining field. Quad bikes are not easy and I will gloss over the traumas of using one; enough to say neither of us will drive one again.

Fitting the penstock pipe into the trench along the old track was relatively easy, but once the route turned down the steep incline it became scarily difficult. At every joint Ian would phone me and I would scamper up the mountain in order to help. The pipe is very heavy and determined to get down the mountain as fast as possible, so at different points they were secured by tying them to trees and posts. The joining process involved fitting huge compression joints. Because of the desire of the pipe to slide downhill we pulled the upper section out of the trench and laid it along the contour, brought the new section in line and with great effort managed to get the fittings on. As neither of us had pipe grips large enough to go round the fittings we resorted to the old system of using rope and steel bars. Finally the buried pipe reached the top of the orchard and the turbine housing.

Often during the installation of the pipe we would cross over to the other side of the valley to gaze and marvel at the dark red-brown line of the trench snaking its way down the mountainside and the digger looking small and vulnerable at the bottom of it. Now looking from the other side all you can see is the green of the mountain; no sign of the installation is visible. The new intake screens are all but invisible, bedded down into the streams; the deep pipe-trench is filled and grown over; and the turbine house looks like a garden shed. No-one would ever know that we had a hydroelectric installation; it's like having an exciting secret, a secret to be shared with everyone.

During this period Richard, our intrepid engineer, had sort of taken up temporary residence with us having broken up, temporarily as it happened, with his "significant other". On many occasions the house filled with his students from the hydro course he was running at the University of Glamorgan. This was a very rich and rewarding period of the installation as students plied up and down the mountain experimenting with different aspects of the installation. With their help the turbine and generator assembly was installed upon the concrete frame and pad that I had built. The system comprised three different sized nozzles connected via separate pipes to a manifold attached to the end of the penstock.

Meanwhile, we dug the trench down through the orchard and rear garden to take the heavy electrical cable to the rear porch of the house, where the electrical control units were housed. Daffodil bulbs were planted on top of the cable before back-filling. The following spring there was this joyous line of yellow blooms weaving down to the house. A delightful reminder of the job done and a useful piece of mapping.

Dai, the electrician, was busy assembling the electrical control units.

The controller is a sophisticated unit that reads the current voltage and wavelength of the grid and alters the generated electricity to the same wavelength but at a slightly higher voltage so that our power will flow into the grid. The only equipment at the time that did this was a unit designed for photovoltaic cells (solar energy technology). This bright-red box had the great name of Sunny Boy. For wind turbines the same company produced one called Windy Boy; sadly they did not make a Wet Boy.

Photovoltaics generate direct current (DC), and therefore the unit only dealt with DC. A water turbine generates alternating current (AC), so a separate piece of equipment was required to convert our AC supply into DC so that Sunny Boy could then convert it back to AC before adjusting it for the grid (very confusing!).

Then came the great moment in heavy rain when the first nozzle was fitted and the gate valve opened. The roar of water under pressure, the spinning purr of the turbine, the flashing lights of the control unit adjusting the supply; and finally, with an audible clunk, our hydro scheme was connected to the grid. We were exporting electricity!

Over the next day the other two nozzles were connected and opened, driving up the power generated to 3kWh. Over the autumn refinements were added, such as an automatic valve fitted to the largest nozzle that would open and close in response to the amount of water available.

The above is a very condensed account of what was a wonderful and generally extremely enjoyable undertaking. The joy of being able to work outside in this beautiful landscape is not to be understated.

We were constantly asked how much money it would generate; not how much electricity. We answered in all honesty that we had no idea, it wasn't why we had done it. We installed our scheme because we could. Just one of many small gestures to make our tread upon the planet a little lighter. Like buying organic produce not for the taste but for the sustainable principal of working with nature and not against it. It may or may not be considered successful in monetary terms but in terms of community involvement and a demonstration of what can be achieved it is a roaring success.

In November of last year, 2011, we decommissioned our original experimental installation and set up a new system. Using the same penstock, the intakes have been rebuilt and a completely new spear valve, turbine, generator and electrical controls installed in a new turbine house. The system now generates a maximum of 9kW as against the 3.2kW of the old system. Our original scheme was set at 3.3kW as at the time this was the maximum that Western Power would allow to be fed into the grid. Things have moved on since then and with our new transformer there is no limit. For the first two years we generated an average of 15,000kWh per year. During the following twenty months up to the time we commissioned our new scheme we generated 5,000kWh. A very vivid reminder of just how dry the previous winters had been.

I began writing this in February; it is now June. Since November of last year our total generation was 25,000kWh, demonstrating just how efficient the new set-up is (and also how wet the summer of 2012 has been). The sinuous line of daffodils has come and gone, to be replaced by a wild flower meadow. Now gazing down from the turbine house I look over a sea of ox-eye daisies, columbines, foxgloves, speedwell, cranesbills, hogweed and waving grasses. As the rain pours down, is it my imagination or can I really sense the electrical power surging under the flower roots and daffodil bulbs beneath my feet? I think I can. It powers me on to the next project and the next, whatever they may be, but for the moment I have beans to harvest, potatoes to dig and the big barn to rebuild and restore.

11
The Web of Life Community Art Project
Helen Moore

In November 2009, some major life changes had brought me to a new town. I had reached a stage of needing to belong somewhere, and Frome, a market town in northeast Somerset, seemed the perfect place to put down roots. Founded in 685 by the Saxon Bishop Adhelm amidst what was then the luxuriant and extensive Selwood Forest, the town appealed to me for many reasons. I loved its old, quirky streets and buildings, the leat that flows down Cheap Street, the cobbles and independent shops of Catherine Hill. And I knew there to be a dynamic creative community, with many talented artists and writers living and working here.

Sustainable Frome, affiliated to the Transition Towns network, also offered a hub supporting all kinds of environmental activity. Their monthly meetings, opening with a convivial shared meal, had already put me in touch with like-minded people; but it was clear that they had busy lives, and I had none of the shared history that bonded them with each other. Having uprooted myself, my close friends were scattered as far away as Scotland, and so at moments I felt quite lonely, living by myself, and in a long-distance relationship with a new partner in London.

In retrospect, making friends seemed easier when I was younger. Now in my late thirties, I didn't seem to fit with many of the social circles that many people of a similar age moved in; and my choice not to have children meant that ready-made social networks formed through the school-gates were not available. However, I had an idea that I felt could make a difference – from past experience I knew that community arts projects can be a wonderful way to bring people together, and so I began to feel that if I were to lead some such project in Frome, it could be a way for me to establish new friendships, as well as contribute to others' lives.

My time working with the Beltane Fire Society in Edinburgh, putting on large-scale outdoor ritual theatre productions to mark the Celtic wheel of the year, had also given me the knowledge that I was capable of leading such a project. However, in Scotland I had never initiated the activity, but instead had maintained and directed it through pre-established circles.

And so my challenge in Frome was going to be persuading others to trust me enough to come on board with a new idea.

Furthermore, I knew that the project smouldering inside me could be difficult to ignite. How would local people feel about creating a funeral to mark the mass extinction of species currently occurring in our world? As an ecopoet, children's author and Forest Schools leader, I feel passionately about the role of the arts and creativity in exploring ecological issues and ideas, and so a few months earlier in May 2010, I'd been drawn to contribute to an all-night vigil outside Westminster, organised by the Campaign Against Climate Change. After a march through central London, which culminated with various speakers, the vigil comprised a programme of "Art and Empowerment", with a range of environmentally orientated artists making contributions throughout the night. My partner, a fellow poet, and I shared our work around 2am, our voices buffered by the constant roar of traffic. But it was sometime later, and through bleary eyes, that I first encountered Brighton-based Feral Theatre.

In a circle of illuminated tombstones dedicated to various extinct species, I was invited to join their funeral ceremony. I was already aware of some of the facts about extinction – particularly that scientists have named the current epoch as the Sixth Mass Extinction, with the rates at which species are disappearing being much higher than the "background rate" at which extinction would usually occur. And I had even written about the disappearance of the Golden Toad from the Cloud Forests of Costa Rica in one of my children's books. But to engage with the issue in this way – collectively, with people naming and mourning lost species, and with the visual spectacle of these beautiful tombstones, and all the flowers, candles and photographs associated with funerals for family or friends – felt meaningful in ways I could barely articulate.

For weeks after my return to Frome, the experience remained alive within me. I'm the kind of person who frequently experiences all sorts of creative flashes, some of which may not ultimately translate into reality. However, this idea wasn't going away and, because it had become enmeshed with my desire to offer something to my community, which might also benefit me, the idea seemed to have an irresistible energy, and kept nagging for attention.

Soon I found myself enthusing about it at a Sustainable Frome meeting, and also at another group I'd joined, with fellow practitioners of the Work that Reconnects. When I suggested that we create something similar to the funeral in our community, I could feel some sparks of interest, but clearly it would be up to me to fan them enough to fire up the project.

One evening I brought the idea to the local Artists' Café. There the idea awoke quite a buzz, with one artist telling me she'd already created a coffin as part of her MA thesis on death, and another enthusiastic about involving a firm of undertakers and arranging a New Orleans-style jazz funeral procession. But another man told me he'd recently been bereaved and hated the idea. Then, a couple of days later, I received a letter from one of the artists telling me she'd had a change of heart, and felt that it was too depressing, especially given her own parents' closeness to death. Having lost my own father the year before, and with my mother terminally ill with cancer, I could empathise. Nevertheless I felt that addressing extinction in my community through the creation of an artistic funeral ceremony was a powerful idea, which I was reluctant to give up.

Soon word reached me that others felt similarly concerned about the project, and someone else suggested that it was just too ambitious an idea for a small rural town. By mid November 2010 I was growing despondent about ever getting it off the ground. Then during a spell of wintry weather, I came down with flu. My unheated flat was damp and cold, and as I lay alone in bed, feverish and with hallucinated shapes and figures moving in and out of my mind, I was enveloped in a shroud of uncertainty as to how or even whether to proceed.

As body and soul underwent their healing crisis, and I drifted in and out of sleep, a host of doubts assailed me. Could I seriously pull off this project when I had no ready-made network of artists to collaborate with? Perhaps the idea was genuinely more suited to a metropolitan audience with more sophisticated tastes? Was I just being too ambitious? Finally, as the mists cleared and I was beginning to regain my strength, I made a bargain with the Universe – give me a sign! Show me that I should take this project forward, and I will! And so at last I got up and went outside for the first time in a week.

By then a slight thaw had set in, but it was still bitterly cold. As I returned through the stone courtyard towards the flats where I lived, I noticed something unusual by the door. At first I thought it was a child's rubber toy. But then, as I peered closer – taking in its naturalism, the greeny-yellow markings – it jumped, and my heart leapt in surprise. Given my recent delirious states, I could barely believe my eyes. Was I still hallucinating? And if not, what was a Common Frog doing there in the middle of winter? Why wasn't it hibernating?

By the time I'd brought it round to a neighbour's garden, where I thought it might fare better amongst the dead leaves and bushes, it had occurred to me this was indeed the sign I'd asked for, and I mentally dubbed him Hermes, after the messenger god. From that moment on, I felt galvanised as never before by this magical sign, and an image of the Common Frog became a talisman for the project.

In early January 2011, I then found a human ally in a fellow member of the Frome Work that Reconnects group. Meretta Hart believed in what I was trying to achieve, and offered to meet on a weekly basis to mentor me through the project. Another member of the group, Mandy Griffiths, a vegan and passionate animal rights supporter, was also excited by my ideas, and together we began to feel that we could make it happen. Meanwhile Charlie Brandt, the owner of one of Frome's various disused chapels, had offered his space on Sun Street in the heart of the old town. As an artist and former teacher of sculpture, and a man with strong feelings about many of the issues connected with our project, Charlie was keen to see the idea develop. And with a vision of his chapel being regularly used as a community arts space, it seemed that our needs could dovetail. The place required work, but in exchange for doing this, I could use it rent-free.

On a freezing January evening, a small group of us met there for the first time. Lisbet Michelsen, another member of the Work that Reconnects group, came along, as did Annabelle Macfadyen, a fellow community artist similarly inspired by Joanna Macy, and whose experience I knew would be invaluable. Wrapped up tightly in hats, coats and gloves, we sat together and started to vision how and when the project might take place.

It soon became clear that to ensure maximum publicity and participation, it would be best to put on our event during the annual Frome Festival in July. A vision seemed to be coalescing. A neighbour and one-time professional illustrator had already begun developing images of extinct species, which she was painting onto posters below a bold graphic exclaiming "LOST", suggesting a missing pet. It was an inspired idea, which caught others' imaginations and helped to demonstrate the kind of creative responses which the project could provoke.

However, there was still a certain amount of unease in the new group about creating the funeral ceremony itself. Annabelle eventually offered a useful perspective, which was that she felt it needed to be contained within a bigger celebration of the natural world and our relationship with it. She indicated that it would be important to do as much community outreach as possible to engage people with what we were doing. Other members of the steering group suggested going into schools and visiting old people's homes, and perhaps also creating an art exhibition.

By now I was gaining a new perspective on leadership. I'd long since evolved a sense of the various strands of my work being in service of Gaia, but I was beginning to see that in order to be a good leader, I needed to listen carefully to everyone's perspectives, and to some extent become the group's servant. And so in taking on board the widening remit, we hit on the idea of calling our vision the Web of Life Community Art Project.

Then followed five months' steady work. As well as the invaluable support that my weekly meetings with my mentor offered, some early successes buoyed me enormously. The previous summer I'd encountered eco-artist Dave Cooper showing his finely-crafted and often humorous paintings at a gallery in Falmouth. Having kept in touch with him, I was delighted when he agreed to show his work at the proposed Web of Life exhibition, which I planned to open during the ten-day Frome Festival, and in conjunction with the Open Studios trail organised by local artists.

Giles Ford, a local painter, had been inspired to create a large diptych for the show; and Mel Sewell, a local landscape photographer, who had previously felt uncomfortable about the project due to a recent bereavement, was suddenly won round, and offered to show some of his black-and-white studies of the remaining fragments of Selwood Forest. My friend Stephen Magrath, a Bath-based artist exploring the connections between art and biology, also came on board, as did Antonius, a Frome-based graphic novelist, who was keen to make some 3-D work in response to the project's theme.

This artwork would be shown in the chapel's oratorium and foyer, while upstairs in the gallery the steering group envisioned displays of art by schoolchildren and information from environmental groups. Already most of my spare time was going into organising the project, and the prospect of facilitating the schools outreach prompted me to apply for some funding. And so, encouraged that the Heritage Lottery Fund were looking to support projects about biodiversity in the Southwest, Meretta and I sat down with an application form.

Ultimately we were unsuccessful with our bid. However, by the time we received a response to our application, we'd already progressed significantly towards making the project happen, and it was inconceivable that we'd stop. Fortunately, what in other circumstances would have been a major cost – the rental of the exhibition space – had already been waived by the owner, and we'd been given permission to operate under Sustainable Frome's umbrella, which meant that their insurance policy could cover us. However, aside from Meretta and I hoping to be paid for our time, there were going to be other costs incurred. Members of the group had generously offered to loan or use their own resources where possible, but none of us could afford to be out of pocket. So where were we going to get some funds?

From that extraordinary moment when I found Hermes on my doorstep, I'd sensed the project was blessed with an underlying energy-flow, and despite moments of doubt, this proved to be the case. The right people always turned up at opportune moments, and when we were really feeling desperate, an anonymous donor had assisted the project, while a couple of other small, local sources of funding were also obtained – all just enough to keep us going.

Meanwhile, Web of Life steering group members were beginning to focus on developing their own areas of interest – chiefly the funeral ceremony, which a local Interfaith minister, Charles Kemp, had agreed to lead, and the funeral procession preceding it. At our meetings, I'd move between conversations, listening to and encouraging people in their plans. Mandy Griffiths had offered to decorate the chapel, so that as well as being an art gallery, it would serve as a sacred space for the ceremony. And Pat Tayler, a local artist experienced in street theatre, had offered to direct the procession, which she envisaged winding its way through the town centre on the busiest Saturday of the festival, with pallbearers carrying a coffin decorated with images of extinct species. Pat had also sketched an exciting line-up of children dressed as animals, and a dramatic sequence involving hubristic bankers, who would drive the animals under the coffin, and counter-posed by a figure representing Hope, who would restore them to life.

With the vibrant energies of late Spring growth to inspire me, I was soon visiting the seven schools signed up to the project. There I engaged the children in a Web of Life activity, which shows how everything is interconnected. With approximately thirty small people wearing labels to denote the animal, plant or insect they were representing, one child would weave a ball of string back and forth across the circle, connecting each species to its food source, habitat, or predator. Finally, with a complex web anchored to their fingers, I'd invite the children to look at what would happen if one part of the web were to be removed. Seeing the marvellous web collapse in front of their eyes, they were well able to understand the implications of extinction. Afterwards I took the children outside to look for bugs, thus giving them a direct experience of the natural world we'd just been discussing. And from there it was relatively simple to encourage them to create pictures and poems celebrating the natural world, or depicting endangered and extinct species.

Witnessing the children's enthusiasm and passion was frequently uplifting. Then, thanks to Meretta's efforts, we fostered another thread of community outreach which was even more touching – our work with the elderly. Having arranged to visit three residential care homes in Frome, we would arrive with arms full of flowers and herbs from Meretta's garden, as well as collections of objects that might trigger memories and other responses to our questions about how the countryside had changed in the residents' lifetimes. And so offering a bouquet to smell, or passing an old scythe or a dead butterfly in a box around the circle, we'd soon get them talking.

One man reminisced about how, as a boy living in a part of town called Adderwell, there were fields and a dark hole with a spring where adders lurked in summer. Sadly this has now vanished under the foundations of a housing estate. Most of the elderly people we spoke to had noticed significant decreases in numbers of birds and butterflies during their lifetimes, and this was a cause for palpable sorrow. Nevertheless, it was clear how greatly the residents appreciated our visit, and it felt hard to walk away knowing that our outreach was limited to that one occasion.

At many of our steering group meetings, people brought in images and information about extinct or endangered species, which helped to educate us all as we went along. Often they shared a story as to why they felt particularly close to that animal, bird or plant. Mel had lived in Portugal, and so knew all about the critically endangered Iberian Lynx, and the breeding programmes designed to conserve them. Meretta's creature was the Manatee, which often suffers appalling injuries from the blades and rudders of water-skis and motorboats. Others brought in stories of hope – for example, the Large Blue Butterfly, successfully reintroduced into certain areas in the U.K. since its extraordinary symbiotic relationship with Red Ants has been discovered.

Gradually our funeral ceremony was taking shape. We had a large coffin, which Mick Dunk had built from scratch and Mel had painted purple. Mick had also sourced some gold plastic handles, and with this decorative feature adding to its lustre, we were now ready to receive the hand-drawn and painted images of extinct species that a local family was making. Meanwhile, the pallbearers had to practice getting the coffin in through the chapel's doors and vestibule, and my new friend Alex Hart, who'd agreed to play Hope in the procession, sourced a range of furry animal costumes that we could borrow for the children.

By early June, work inside the chapel had begun in earnest. Inevitably with these kinds of projects, there's always more to do than one originally imagines. I was fortunate to have the consistent help of Mick and Mel, who became my right-hand men, and whenever my partner Niall was in town, he too offered his assistance. And so together we spent many long hours clearing the space, cutting and sticking down carpet tiles, repainting walls, and dusting and polishing the pews upstairs in the gallery.

Our flyers had been designed and printed, and we distributed these to as many willing volunteers as we could find to display in shop windows and on notice boards around town. By now our series of "LOST" posters had also come to include images of species that had been successfully conserved, such as the Large Blue Butterfly. These were entitled "FOUND", whilst other posters were inscribed with "GOING, GOING" to represent critically endangered species, like the Orangutan from the rainforests of Sumatra, and the Ashy-faced Owl from the islands of Hispaniola and Tortuga in the Caribbean. Finally, the series of nearly twenty species was complete, and these beautiful A4 sized, hand-drawn posters were photocopied and mounted on cardboard. Overnight they appeared around the town attached to lampposts and street signs. There was even a Golden Toad squatting on the Market Cross.

With one week to go, the chapel was ready to become a gallery, and the artists arrived with their paintings, photographs, and sculptures. The various schools involved had also completed their displays, and, as each was delivered to me at the chapel, I was thrilled to see what the children had created. In particular I loved their ardent messages directed at grown-ups, such as: "Don't kill hedgehogs!" Of note was a tapestry created by the local group of home-educated children. Using recycled textiles, it depicted a range of extinct and endangered animals, including a deliciously tactile Giant Panda and a Pink River Dolphin with a charming smile. A year and a half on, it still hangs in Frome Library.

At last the project was taking on a life of its own, as all well-managed projects should. I remember clearly the moment when I saw that it no longer depended on me. One evening, knowing that various groups were meeting at the chapel, I decided to drop in to see how everything was going. As I approached I could hear singing emanating from within. Entering unnoticed, I heard for the very first time the choir rehearsing a hymn I'd written. Guy Wilson, a talented local musician, had set it to music, and the exquisite harmonies filled me with tears of joy and awe.

Under Mandy's expert direction, we soon added the final touches to the space with small shrines, drapes, framed photographs of extinct and endangered species, candles and vases of fresh flowers. We held a small launch party for the opening of the exhibition, and three days later, the culmination of the Web of Life Community Art Project came with the event I'd so long imagined – Frome's own funeral for extinct species.

I woke filled with anticipation and anxiety. Would it rain? Would anyone turn up? But in the early afternoon, the sun was blazing down on our heads, and when I approached the meeting place for the procession outside St. John's Church, there were people gathering in all kinds of costumes, some with homemade placards.

At last the coffin was lifted onto the pallbearers' shoulders, and we set off to the slow beat of drums and the tune of a lone clarinet, accompanied by growls from children in furry costumes. Meanwhile our spoof bankers – Sir Clarence and Ricky, representing old and new money – chuffed on cigars and spewed the most self-serving and outrageously anti-environmental commentary they could muster.

Glory be to Gaia

Helen Moore

Guy Wilson

For rain bows, gla-ciers and fresh snow. We ho nour and praise you Gai - a. Mys te rious blue pla net

U - nique in this vast u ni verse. Like your wi-dest ri -vers our hearts flow with gra ti-

tude. Glo-ry be to Gai - a. For fo rests val leys and ex qui site flowers.

Great Mo ther. Thank you for clean air and wa - ter. and all the fruits and seeds ma ni fest

through your a bun dant power. For bird song, moun tains and clear lakes. Gi -ant pul sa-ting orb of life,

From which we have grown. Please help us feel our in ter de pendence with all a -ni-mal and human kind.

For in sects worms and all ti ny creatures. Cease-less wheel of life. We embrace your e-ter nal cy cle. The rich

soil our bo-dies will be - come, and the gift this pre sent mo-ment is. For whales phospho re scence and

fish. Pla -net jewel of the cos mos. Sa-cred be ing in-fused in our D N

A Please light the spark of peace in us, that we may serve this pre-cious Life.

Glo-ry be to Gai - a. Glo-ry be to Gai - a. Glo-ry be to Gai - a.

Glo-ry be to Gai - a. Glo-ry be to Gai - a. Glo ry be to Gai - a.

Under a banner proclaiming: "PROTECT THE WEB OF LIFE! EXTINCTION IS FOREVER!" a colourful ribbon of people wound its way up the steep cobbles of Catherine Hill. Residents hung out of windows to see what was happening; shopkeepers peered from their doorways; and passers-by snapped pictures. Although there was a sombre quality to our procession, it was simultaneously infused with humour and the sheer joy that comes when a group of people responds creatively to an issue that has touched their hearts. From time to time Hope, dressed in white, would emerge from amidst the procession and to loud cheers, would banish the bankers before restoring the animals to life.

Arriving at the doors of Sun Street Chapel, the pallbearers manoeuvred the coffin inside. As they entered, people were given an order of service and a small tissue paper cut-out bearing the name of a creature or plant that is no longer part of the tapestry that makes this uniquely diverse Earth. The mellow strains of a harp filled the space, and a group of female "Earth Guardians" dressed in turquoise ushered people to their seats. I was astonished to see so many had come – soon even the freshly-polished pews of the upper gallery were full.

Charles Kemp, our Interfaith minister, introduced the ceremony, and there followed waves of music, poetry and storytelling that took people on a journey into gratitude, sorrow, awe at the complex history of life on our planet, and culminated with a sense of what we each could do to make a difference. Parents rocked children in their arms; young and old sat listening intently; and the choir sang praises to Gaia.For the central ritual in the ceremony, the Earth Guardians moved amongst the assembled crowd to collect up the tissue paper shapes representing nearly two hundred extinct species...

Glaucous Macaw, Pyrenean Ibex, Javanese Lapwing, Ratas Island Lizard, Bush Wren, Downy Hemp Nettle, Moa, Zanzibar Leopard, Vine Raiatea Tree Snail, Bachmann's Warbler, Norfolk Damselfly, Red-bellied Gracile Mouse Opossum, Grand Cayman Thrush, Yangtze River Dolphin, Utah Lake Sculpin, Flame Brocade Moth, Bory's White Bat, Passenger Pigeon, Silver Trout, South China Tiger...

These were put in bowls of spring water and placed on the coffin. The water represented our tears, and the floating candles that were lit in the top of each bowl, the spirits of the departed. Looking around the faces of this gathered crowd of new friends, acquaintances and members of my local community, I could see those tears. But unexpectedly this was not a moment for me to grieve. Instead I noticed a smile spreading inside my heart. Together with all these people who'd gifted their time and energy, I'd accomplished my vision. Like a pebble cast into a stream, it would ripple outwards from here and now. But the knowledge of its effects would be the preserve of future generations.[1]

Note to Chapter 11

1   A video of the Web of Life Community Art Project by Adrian Strong can be found at *http://www.frome.tv/2011/07/community-wide-environment-art-project-launches-frome-festival/*

12
Discovering that
We Live in an Ancient and Beautiful Universe
Helena Kettleborough & Nora Kettleborough

Starting our journey: of stuff and stars

To start at the beginning, dreamer and geologian Thomas Berry says that we modern humans have no adequate story to give meaning to our lives and place us in our world.[1] We have a story but it's very one sided: you go to school, you get a job, you work and you buy stuff. Then you die. The trouble with this story is that it's not satisfying. There's no oomph in it. It's not the whole story either; there is more. The real story, as modern science shows us, began a long time ago. As cosmologist Brian Swimme tells it, "You take hydrogen gas and you leave it alone and it turns into rosebushes, giraffes and humans."[2]

This is again only a partial version. It has taken a long time, 13,700,000,000 years, to get to hummingbirds, bluebells and oak trees. Another way of telling the story is Joanna Macy's advice to us "to act our age". We operate on very short timescales of maybe a few or twenty years when already the CO2 we've put into the atmosphere will be around for over 100,000 years. We think in small periods of time, not like the hydrogen atoms that we are, billions of years old. One way to learn our age is to go on a journey individually and together. My youngest daughter Nora and I want to share with you living in the universe, not as an abstract idea but as a foundation for our lives and a basis for caring for each other.[3] I (Helena) share how I came to appreciate the universe we live in, bringing up our family of three daughters in our street and I (Nora) share how I perceive this thinking about our place in the universe. Through experiences of climbing three mountains, I suggest how the universe can only be as big as the love we have for each other in our own lives.

It started with a tree

I've lived for many years in an inner city area of Manchester on a diverse street with people with family roots in Pakistan, Germany, America, Iran, Bangladesh, Ireland, France, Spain, London, Nottinghamshire and

Lancashire. Like many inner-city residents, I often got fed up of the rubbish, unkempt gardens and the fact that no-one seemed to care. We had a go at moving, which didn't work out, and decided to stay and put our energy into our local area with our fellow neighbours. One of the first things we did was to plant street trees, which isn't as easy as it sounds, as permission is needed for each street tree outside someone's house. It involved leafleting and door knocking. The delight was we could all choose our own tree. We went for hawthorn, rowan, cherry and silver birch. Soon we had thirteen little saplings on our street.

One of the best things about building our street is that we're growing a community for our children. At Christmas we decided we'd decorate the trees and put shiny baubles up with the help of a handful of neighbours. Three years later, we had twelve children and ten adults, cake, baubles and silver strands for the bases of the trees. Many other good things have happened. We've had three street parties, closing the road and putting tables down the middle. Last year's was in the rain. There we were, standing in the street, eating pakoras, with the rain streaming down. Only in England, we said as we tucked into soggy cake. We set up a book club and now some of the children want their own. We meet for Big Tidy Ups and finish with tea and refreshments, growing our community with care. As Thomas Berry says, everything in the universe is connected to everything else. By acting in communion, we start to build ourselves back into the fabric of the universe.

It's hard, living in the inner city, to get a sense of growing up in something bigger than ourselves. The stars in the sky are faint – only by looking up very closely do a small number twinkle out on a clear night. The horizon is hemmed in by buildings. In the 1990s, when our children were young, we were in a recession and burglaries were common in our area. One night, a burglar stole our TV. We decided not to replace it. Why? I'd been reading the *Hidden Heart of the Cosmos*[4] in which Brian Swimme suggested that some of the brightest and cleverest minds in our society were telling our children unwanted stories, stories about buying things and if they bought things they'd be happy. At the time it was estimated that children would see 100,000 of these stories during their childhood. So we decided to try and bring our children up without some of these messages.

Six leaps around our cosmic neighbourhood

A few years after our TV was stolen, it was the Millennium. The post softly thudded through the letterbox. The girls ran to the door and scooped up the mail. I opened the National Geographic Millennium Special. Inside was a map of our neighbourhood, our cosmic neighbourhood. I sat still and studied the colourful A3 map.[5] The map makers recommended taking "leaps of scale" around our neighbourhood.

I imagined taking these six leaps around our universe. From our solar system to the nearest star, Alpha Centauri is one leap, 4.3 light years. From our nearest star to the local group of stars is the next leap. It includes Orion and all the bright stars we know and love. The next leap is from our nearest stars to the Milky Way galaxy itself, our neighbourhood, our home. From our galaxy to our nearest galaxy Andromeda is the 4th leap, a leap of 2.5 million light years. Andromeda and the Milky Way pin-wheel round each other every 250 million years. From Andromeda to our nearest galaxies, the local group is the next step. And finally, from our local group of galaxies to the Cosmos itself. I put the poster up in our bedroom. And there it stayed over the decade. I mentally follow this path many times. If I am ever down-hearted, I travel the cosmos on these six leaps and feel again the grandeur of the universe.

A universe story

A year or so after the Millennium my partner Phil agreed to lead a universe walk through our local park, Birchfields.[6] We started outside the community centre. We celebrated the big bang with the youngest and oldest members of the group popping two balloons with a fork and then set off. For the first billions of years, nothing much seemed to happen, galaxies formed and then wow! The supernova that created all the elements for life on Earth appeared. "Yes," Phil told us, "we are all made of stardust." We stopped by a flower. "See this pattern?" Phil asked. "All the patterns on the planet are repeated in the universe: the swirling head of a sunflower and the swirling spiral galaxies." We were over two-thirds through our walk and it was only then that planet Earth appeared. We kept going. Single-cell life arrived and then two billion years later the first multi-cellular organisms. Back outside the community centre again and we arrived at the great explosion of life which began sixty-five million years ago resulting in whales and chimpanzees and giraffes and roses. It was only in the last tiny fraction of the final step that all of human history took place. We found the treasure at the end of the story – conscious life of which we have the gift – and celebrated with small bars of fair trade chocolate.

Throwing the ball…back into the past and into the future…

The universe isn't just enormous, it's very ancient. Just how ancient is hard to imagine, but I try. It was summertime and we, as part of the global diaspora, were going on our holidays. Some of our neighbours were going home to Spain and France, others to Pakistan and Germany. We went with our family in Ireland on a walk. We started on the Iveragh Peninsula on an ancient Mass pass in the Kingdom of Kerry, following in the steps of my ancestors who, in centuries gone by, walked up this mountain and down again to go to church every Sunday.

We climbed up and could see across Dingle Bay and the hump-back silhouette of the Blasket Islands. As we climbed higher, two lakes appeared below, in a perfect U-shaped valley formed by glaciers thousands of years ago. The ice has gone, leaving behind grey, still waters and boulders scattered down the mountainside. To the top and over the peak we got a breathtaking view: down the Ferta valley to the town of Cahersiveen. The valley before us was covered in the green and brown fields of Kerry: stone walls crisscrossing the landscape. We sat for lunch and watched the view. At our feet, moss, bog flowers, and insects crawled by. Idly, I noticed a small piece of rock and picked it up, seeing to my delight the ripples of an ancient beach clearly etched on the stone. A visit to the Barracks Museum in Cahersiveen informed us that our piece of rock was likely to be 320 million years old.

I imagined throwing a ball back towards that sea which once covered Iveragh. I let my mind wander freely to the sea, older than mammals, older than dinosaurs. I imagined myself throwing the ball over eons and eons. And then instead I thought forward, forward 320 million years into the future. Beyond the 50,000 year time span that the stars will form the Orion constellation, beyond the encounter the solar system will have with a travelling star a million years into the future. As far as my mind could imagine.

A week later I returned to my inner-city home and local neighbourhood. I kept in my mind the age of the unimaginably old beach and I thought forward again. I sensed that we need people who can begin to relate to the Earth in a new way: understand that the Earth and the universe we live in is very old. And alive. We require people who can move confidently between the great age and splendour of our beautiful and ancient universe and can work to create better communities, in the here and now. I put my little piece of sandstone rock as a centrepiece on our kitchen table, a symbol of a promise for the past and the future.

Our one and only home: Saturn and our pale blue orb

In Autumn 2010 our youngest daughter left home. Nora enrolled for the Astrophysics Society at university, who gave her a copy of the picture of the Earth taken by the Cassini spacecraft from Saturn, at a distance of 930 million miles from the Earth. Nora took the picture and left and then turned round and got another copy. When I met Nora two months later she took out a folder and handed me a present: "For you," she said. I stared at the picture, mesmerised. It is a glorious full-colour portrait of Earth, our home planet. The spacecraft has turned from looking out into the farthest reaches of the solar system back towards the sun and her home planet. Saturn blocks out the light of the sun, so Cassini is able to take a picture of Earth. It is not a picture of Earth as we normally see her, with her beautiful swirling white clouds and numinous blue skies. No, it is a tiny pixel, barely a dot outside one of Saturn's rings. Staring hard, it is possible to see Earth as a tiny pale blue orb of haunting beauty. As cosmologist Carl Sagan said, this tiny point of blue light is "the only home we've ever known".

Wandering stars

Our eldest daughter, Merry, teaches nursery-age children. We went on holiday together at the October half term, spending time gathering acorns for her school nature table. For Christmas, her new partner gave me a large box, which I opened with great interest. Inside, amongst the wrapping paper, was a large yellow ball. I pulled it out and found eight other tiny balls, one with rings: it was a miniature solar system. Jupiter and the big red spot, tiny Mercury so close to the sun. With the click of a switch, they started slowly circling around each other and around the sun. Earth's siblings, who've been so important in our history: Saturn, Jupiter and Neptune kept the mighty rocks away from Earth when she was young, allowing life to take hold.

A month later and Jupiter, Venus and Mars were visible in the heavens above us. For once, from our street in Manchester we got a nearly perfect view. Mars high in the night sky overhead, a distinctly red twinkling moving dot. Jupiter a dazzling bright light in the sky, moving in front of our door as the evening progressed. Venus ethereal and beautiful close to the moon. It was such a wonderful sight that I took to stopping neighbours in the street and asked, "Have you seen the planets?" "No," they said, or "I thought they were just stars." I pointed them out and together, we stood and wondered.

A spirit for the tasks ahead

Does it matter that I live on my street or in my planet or in our neighbourhood, the Milky Way galaxy? Writer Peter Reason travelled to America to see Thomas Berry and asked him why it was so important that we live in the universe. Thomas Berry, an old man by then, replied that we will need great psychic energy for the task ahead and we will get that energy from the cosmos. So it's very important we live in communion with the stars and planets. What do we learn from our ancient and beautiful universe? We learn that life itself is very special. In the vast reaches of space, Planet Earth and all her creatures are to be treasured and taken care of. In terms of geological time, humans are very young. We potentially have a long history in front of us if we can get through the next period. Thinking about the sandstone rock and the length of time back to 320,000,000 years ago gives me a better appreciation of what it means to say that humanity is causing the sixth biggest mass extinction in 4,500,000,000 years. Extinction is forever; no creature made extinct will ever come back.

The recession returned and burglaries increased again. The campaign for a million green jobs came to Manchester as part of a nationwide tour. The family gathered again to celebrate our middle daughter Ita's graduation. I was struggling with the empty nest syndrome. The house was quiet. The music was turned off. There were no friends calling round. No more taxi driving to do. Well into her second year of university, our youngest daughter Nora gave me a call: would we be her support team for the Three Peaks Challenge?

From one generation to another

When my mum came back from the first workshop and asked me if I would like to work with her on this chapter and include some of my own story, I thought it would be too difficult to put into words. Then my father suggested a recent expedition involving three mountains might be a good way to frame my thoughts. It was a journey with friends; a challenge to climb three of the highest peaks in Great Britain in the space of twenty-four hours. But it somehow managed to be much more than that. It demonstrated what I had gained from an upbringing by parents – particularly my mum – with a different way of seeing the world.

What my mum has tried to instil in me from the moment I was born is an appreciation of the world we live in, not only of the planet we call home but of our place in the universe as a whole. She has brought me and my sisters up in a cosmos of great age and size, not just in a home, and she has shared her personal intellectual and spiritual journey with us. The names Matthew Fox and Thomas Berry have been in my vocabulary as long as I can remember, and though for a long time I didn't really know who they were, I recognised that to my mum they were as Harry Potter was to me… and still are, in both cases. So ok, we've never had a TV. Well we did, until it got stolen when I was about four. Playground conversations about the latest programme always passed me by, and the question "so what's all your furniture pointing at?" was proved to be not only a joke from Friends, but a real life mystery to many people. And for that I can thank another big name in mum's field, Brian Swimme, and his views on the "brainwashing" that is television advertising. Though only an example, that specific case has probably been one of the larger factors that have made my life on an everyday level feel different to that of others my age. And how has this upbringing shaped my world view? Let's get back to the Peaks.

Climb the highest mountain in each of Scotland, England and Wales in a continuous period of 24 hours. Sound appealing? For many, I guess not. I've always enjoyed the outdoors, probably stemming from experiences in the Kerry Mountains in Ireland, but it wasn't until I went to university and mentioned my interest in the Three Peaks Challenge[7] that I suddenly found we were doing more than talking about it. We had set a date. Four second-year physics students, two willing chauffeurs in the form of my parents and plenty of naïve optimism: we set off one Friday in April. Our arrival in the Scottish Highlands was my first indication that I was going to be blown away. I think it was the magnitude of the mountains, that and the realisation that we were planning on climbing the tallest of them all.

We spent the evening going over map skills, compass reading and triple checking the guide book. Six in the morning arrived and, after much less sleep than intended, we set off. The twenty-four hours had begun.

One mountain, so many lifetimes: Ben Nevis

A single path runs up Ben Nevis, popularly known as The Pony Track;
this route is 17 kilometres long, up and down,
and includes 1352 metres of ascent.

It doesn't take long to start sweating when climbing Ben Nevis. There's no build-up really – you cross a bridge and then it's straight on up. After weeks of dreary weather the skies cleared for us and it was such a blessing. For several hours it was just us four and the mountains, suddenly part of the scenery rather than simply onlookers. As we reached the snow line at roughly 900m, the cold really started to set in and our legs were beginning to complain. At least the clear weather meant that tracks from the day before had not been obliterated so navigation was easier, though we still checked the map frequently. The elation once we reached the summit was like one I've rarely felt before.

When in 1771 James Robertson made the first recorded climb to the summit, he saw the same view. These mountains have stood tall and watched human history unfold over a time period that is nothing compared to how long they have been there before us.

When you stand up there at that trig point, knowing that at that moment you're the highest, tallest person in the British Isles, it's hard not to feel that connection with the planet, and your place in it. We need to appreciate what we've got, because what we've got is absolutely incredible. Looking down on the world from 1343 metres, it's easier to recognise how imperative it is to protect the gift that we've been given, and not let our selfishness and ignorance destroy the precious planet we live on. After all, it's the only one we've got.

Sunrise and sunset: Scafell Pike

The Wasdale Head route is 9.6 kilometres long, up and down,
and includes 989 metres of ascent.

A drive, some patches of sleep and a lot of chocolate later, we arrived in the Lake District on a cool, fresh evening. By the time we started the ascent, almost everybody else was coming down – I have never climbed a mountain at dusk before. While Scafell Pike is the highest that England has to offer, it's not the most conventionally beautiful. Very rocky the entire way up, the best views were provided by the setting sun across Wastwater. So here, I wanted to stop and think for a minute. Solar systems are born from supernovae – the rotating remains of extinct stars. Most of the mass is pulled into the central star, in our case the Sun, while extra remnants form planets, moons and belts, all still revolving around their axes as well as orbiting that central star. As Earth moves, that rotation is observed by us in the rising and setting of the Sun – each and every day, this occurrence is a reminder of our position in the universe, of our place in the larger scheme of things. If we only recognise it.

Though relieved to get to the top of Scafell Pike, we didn't hang around long. It was cold and there was little daylight left. And if it wasn't for one of my friends having his head screwed on just that bit tighter than the rest of us, we might have descended into the wrong valley – perhaps we can't always succeed in things on our own. A quick check of the map and we were corrected, free to descend as speedily as possible into the growing darkness.

Darkness and the elements: Snowdon

The Pyg track includes a distance of 11 kilometres, up and down,
and an ascent of 723 metres.

This final stretch in North Wales was by far the most demanding, though by this stage as much mentally as physically. In our sleep-deprived state we zipped up our waterproofs, ready to face not only the cold of night but some of the strongest winds I have ever experienced. Head-torches guiding our way, stopping often to check our route, we climbed Snowdon as dawn arrived and reached its peak virtually to the minute of the 24 hour mark. It was an intense experience – persuading our legs to keep going in darkness like nothing you get in the city. The highest point of the mountain is very exposed and the force of the winds swirling round the summit meant that it just eluded us. About two metres below, clinging to the rock face, was as high as any of us dared to climb but the fun we had trying to get higher eclipsed any disappointment.

We had one minor low point on the trip. Because of the unbelievably strong winds on Snowdon and the steepness of the path, we made the decision to descend by a different route. As it was we were still buffeted like we'd never been buffeted before, but the steady descent was undoubtedly the safer option. However, we were unable to tell my parents of the change in plan. By the time we arrived, we were much later than expected and my mum had been harbouring fears that took a while to fade. Despite the immensity of her thinking, the love of our lives is immediate and specific.

Her love for the planet and the universe is the basis of this entire worldview, and crucially the recognition of our place in it. It is love for all that has passed which means that we are here today, and all that will pass. But this worldview by no means forgets the present and so we must love and cherish what we have right now at this moment, both on the universal scale and on that of our own personal adventures. So if that means that I have to put up with mum stressing about me from time to time, I think I can handle it.

Often around my friends I would refer to my mum as "wacky", it was the excuse I would use to explain away the washing up of tin foil, the spiders who were as welcome in our kitchen as any guest and the barnacles who were our cousins. And I never dared to tell many about the, for want of a better phrase, Earth rituals. But without travelling far, we experienced so many elements in that single day; the snow, the rocks, the wind. Each mountain brought us something different, showed us some new aspect of the wonder that is Planet Earth. Even Scafell, with its perhaps less stunning views, properly connects us to the ancient rocks which shape the planet. Formed roughly 450 million years ago, the summit boulder field is so ancient compared to our meagre number of years whether we're talking about me or my Granny. And that's nothing at all on the age of the universe. I guess what I'm trying to express is the recognition that, now I'm older, these quirks about my mum are things I am more comfortable with, and have come to respect.

Back in the rush of the city it's easy to forget just how close these wonders are. My mum can look at a tadpole in the back garden and find in that so much pleasure, knowing that the cosmos is all interconnected. For me, it takes the feeling of being on top of the world you get from climbing a mountain to feel quite such a connection with the universe, but the fascination I find in studying physics must also stem from this inherited joy of the world. Here lies the difference between me and my friends; they haven't had the opportunity to share in these things. Now I feel that perhaps it would benefit others to grow up thus, in light of the "tasks ahead" as my mum puts it.

Living in an ancient and beautiful universe: life is very special
On the rare occasion of a cloudless night just above Kells Bay, Co. Kerry, you can see the Milky Way. Amongst thousands of other stars, the bright band of the spiral is visible to the naked eye, and is a spectacular sight to see. We sit as a family and discuss the collision of Andromeda with the Milky Way in 5,000,000,000 years' time. By then our street community in Manchester will be more ancient than the most ancient of history. But the adoption of six hedgehogs from a local rescue centre and the sponsorship of mountain gorillas by a group of children will remain an important event. No act is too small. Holding our piece of sandstone rock, we set off on our six leaps around the universe again harnessing the love as we go. For though on a universal scale the Earth is so very small, who could imagine a universe without all of its children.

Notes to Chapter 12

1   Berry, T, 1988. *The Dream of the Earth.* San Francisco: Sierra Club; Berry, T, 1999. *The Great Work: Our Way into the Future.* New York: Bell Tower

2   *http://www.enlightennext.org/magazine/j34/swimme1.asp?page=2,* accessed 18th July 2012. See also Swimme, BT, & Tucker, ME (2011). *The Journey of the Universe.* New Haven: Yale University Press

3   Thank you to Jane Riddiford for this framing.

4   Swimme, B, 1999. *Hidden Heart of the Cosmos: Humanity and the New Story.* New York, Orbis Books

5   *http://i36.photobucket.com/albums/e18/Railman2/Geographic%20 maps/ April%2023/N240TheUniverseOct1999b.jpg,* accessed 2nd August 2012

6   Colebrook, E. and Colebrook, M, 2000. *Walking the Sacred Story, A New Ritual for Celebrating the Universe.* Available as download from *http://www.greenspirit.org.uk/resources/WalkingTheStory.shtml*

7   *www.thethreepeakschallenge.co.uk*

13

Cabbages & Cranes:
Weaving Together People and Possibility
Jane Riddiford
with Gabrielle Harding, Lilienne Isebor,
Toyosi Adebenojo & Silvia Pedretti

I am part of Global Generation, hence, part of nature and developing life to create a sustainable future. It's an amazing experience to be part of a community and have a common interest with others.
Gabrielle, 15 years

Global Generation's (GG) home is in an old bus car park in the middle of one of the largest development sites in Europe. More than a thousand hands have converted a concrete slab into an abundant and portable oasis. The process of creating vegetable gardens in a series of skips (dumpsters) began in 2009. "The Skip Garden" as it is known, is a natural extension to our work of re-framing cities and who we are in them. We have also created gardens in school grounds and on the roofs of office buildings.

Back in 2004 when we were setting up GG, I (Jane) often had the sense that we were uncovering a map of connectedness that was already there; just not visible. It has been an instinctive process that has often felt like listening to a whispering in the wind. People involved in GG's work have also been struck by the energy that connects seemingly disparate elements like youth and business...cabbages and cranes.

Something exists and is growing already. Separate parts joining together, already connected, but loosely.
Anita Sadler, Argent Kings Cross

Kings Cross, where most of GG's work is based, is a bit like a sandwich. On either side are the people who live in the area, some of them for one or two generations at most. In the middle is disused railway land, the size of 67 football fields. Now new offices, a university, and accommodation have been built. Big business is moving in. It could all too easily stay an out-of-bounds area for the many people who live there. Supporting local youngsters to become catalysts for positive change is at the heart of the work. We call our voluntary youth leaders Generators; 14 – 19 year olds like Gabrielle, Tyosi and Lilienne who have contributed to this chapter. There are about 50 Generators, girls and boys, regularly involved. GG's ethos is about doing and learning together; planting vegetables and sharing a meal, looking after bees on the rooftop of a nearby office building. In a spirit of two-way learning our workshops involve youngsters working alongside the workers who come in and out of Kings Cross by day. Many of the workers are involved in constructing the roads and buildings in this new part of London; others work for the media companies who are moving into the area.

Practical activity is bookended with time for reflection. Even though we are in one of the noisiest parts of London we introduce participants to a practice of silence and stillness that we call "sitting still", sometimes in a circle and sometimes individually dotted around the Skip Garden. We have found that silence combined with Freefall writing[1] is a helpful way of bypassing limiting ideas; a chance to hear and tell the story of more than the world of *things*. We have been heartened by the willingness of young and old to experience and express themselves in new ways. All of the contributions in this chapter were written through this process.

The discussion of values is an important ingredient in our method. Like nutrients that make a garden grow, the exchange of meaning and values is what makes culture develop. A session in the Skip Garden often begins with participants introducing themselves to each other by selecting and speaking about a value that is important to them. It is a way of encouraging people to show the best part of themselves. Despite initial reticence, time and time again we have witnessed barriers drop and the energy in a group transform.

All I remember is arriving at the Skip Garden and being met by a portacabin full of construction workers. I wasn't impressed. I remember that I was so cynical and unmotivated. Then we were set a task, to partner up and get to know each other. What could I say? What couldn't I say, it's like we were from two different worlds. Disbelief, this wasn't going to work out. I mean I didn't need to talk to them, so I guessed I wouldn't. We sat in a big round tent with my Lithuanian partner by my side. I didn't say a word. It wasn't until the values cards were introduced and we had to explain them to each other...wow! This guy was deep. I got the chance to look behind the disguises of a construction site and realise that someone like me could talk to someone like him. We were somewhat alike. It was time to break the barrier. Global Generation can say they've broken a

barrier too. They've merged what you would think was a dream and made it a reality. I've learnt to believe in the unbelievable and break the barrier.
Lilienne Isebor, 16 years

The atmosphere created between people in these settings is potent. Whilst hard to measure and define, it is I believe key to Global Generation's success in encouraging the young people and the businesses we work with to share our vision and our sense of optimism.

A young person's journey with Global Generation often begins at our campsite on Pertwood organic farm in Wiltshire. The enthusiasm expressed after a few days on camp has inspired a number of our business collaborators to also come to Pertwood. Nonetheless actually getting the camps off the ground has been nerve-wracking work. Many of the young people we work with have never left London, slept outdoors or seen the stars at night.

The day before we left for one of the camps, our Youth Manager Nicole van den Eijnde called me. "The weather forecast is for rain and gale-force winds. What do we do? Half the Generators have bailed out; they're not coming to Pertwood, we are five down." We both took a deep breath, knowing it is often the parents who are nervous to let their children go. We also knew that the site is sheltered, so I said "Let's give it one more shot… we are too far in to cancel. Put the word out wider and see what happens." As I walked away from the phone, I thought of the forming and reforming nature of creativity. I was surprised at my own trust in the situation. These moments of uncertainty have been well worth it.

I am sitting here in the wide expanse knowing that I am not in control of anything around me but I know I am safe because it is peaceful and every aspect of nature works in harmony.
Lilienne Isebor

Being at Pertwood, sitting around the fire was a new experience for me. I was in the countryside with no technology, with a bunch of strangers. (Who would soon become family.) Yet it was so amazing, the bonds between the members of the group were being formed right away, at that very moment, within the noise of conversation and excitement. That spirit of togetherness was forever present and highlighted as we sat in a circle basking in the warmth of the glowing fire. I felt at one with not only nature but everyone around me…

I helped to start the fire. This involved getting logs and branches from the shed and putting them in the little fire hole that had been set out. Then we had to light the fire while the wind whipped at our faces and the flame on the match.

With Global Generation you often end up doing a lot of things that you never would have thought about doing. Like sleeping in a tent full of insects miles away from London, from home and everything you know.
Tyosi Abedonojo

We still run the campsite; however, perhaps most significant is the effect GG's work is having in the changing area of Kings Cross. It is not an accident but a deliberate choice to be based here. We have discovered that a construction site is a potent place in which to enliven people with the process of change. Along with its rich harvest of vegetables (which young people sell to local restaurants), the Skip Garden has provided a safe space for participants (local young people, construction workers, designers and Bengali mothers), who often hold different world views (traditional, modern, postmodern), to ask questions…big questions.

It was the 14th of March 2011 when I left snakes, millipedes, poison dart frogs and tigers in the zoo where I was working, to move to London. I was scared. I grew up in Italy surrounded by endless Zea maize fields and cows, having the ploughed ground constantly colouring the creases of my hands. I was scared to lose myself, my nature, to never find again what we all seem to be searching for: the reason of why we are here on this planet and what to do with this life. I was afraid to freeze the enquiry that I have been cultivating since I was young thanks also to the written words of men and women in the open universe of philosophy. But the 10th of May 2011, in the middle of a construction site, in an old dusty gazebo, I met the people that gave me the chance to believe that a city couldn't stop my enquiry but actually could make it more vibrant. I remember my first step into one of their movable skip gardens. Someone like me was there: someone that didn't want to be just a dreamer but part of a post-modern form of activism and education, which is not a battle against something but it is a look inside, it is a "doing" which is not separation but connection, interdependence and also a fusion with silence.

And now little more than a year later I am a facilitator on the Generator programme. I often wonder how it is people so young can write such amazing stories? It starts with sitting in a circle, around the fire in the yurt, in the Skip Garden. I feel close to them in these circles where there is no age. When the world around us breathes, moves, carries on, we are there together, so far away from the hot centre of the Earth but so close to our self. Did you hear that loud scream? Oh it is just a spider coming down the roof! Someone saw a flying insect and he's running away. The Generators are there to remind me that the dialogue is the key, the circle. It is the circle of generations, ideas, planets, movements and stillness in all that is there. The Pertwood smell of cow manure, the bird song beneath the traffic in Kings Cross…the carbonium

and nitrogen everywhere. There is everything in one thing and one thing is connected with everything.
Silvia Pedretti, GG Project Facilitator

Just as we have learnt to create the right soil conditions to grow plants in hard places, we have learnt that it is from the relationships between people that a new and more responsible culture will emerge. In skips and poly-tunnels with paper and pencil our collaborators find the words for more than can be seen.

No-one can "build" a community. But what we can do is provide the right conditions for a community to grow. What I experience on this site is the nurturing of those conditions and connections. What we can do is make links, build trust, get to know each other and inevitably the rest will happen. Once the right conditions are in place plants cannot but grow. We have to trust in the wisdom of a plant, that it knows how to grow…and so do we if the conditions are right. I feel what I am doing here is an adventure. It is exciting and the end result is uncertain, but that is okay.
Angela Jewell, Argent Kings Cross.

On a good day the process of bringing life to this new part of London seems as if it is happening by itself. So much so that I often forget what it has taken to turn ideas into concrete realities. There have been many late nights filling in grant applications and risk assessments, all needed to work with "minors" on a construction site. At times I wondered if the potential I sensed was a figment of my imagination and if the numbers on my spreadsheets would really bear fruit. I often feel the need to be bilingual. Promising to deliver on fixed outputs and outcomes, whilst knowing that the beauty of GG's work is that our vision emerges in the footsteps of shared commitment. We are grateful for Lottery and Local Authority funding that has made the work possible and heartened by the fact that they have been flexible enough to recognise that our promises were likely to "evolve". Many of our investors have said they have provided funds because they saw the commitment and sense of purpose in the young people who are involved with us.

Nature continuously changes, grows and develops. I was quite a pessimistic person and Global Generation has helped me to refresh myself and think positively of my surroundings and what I can do to benefit myself and those around me. We are not subscribing to the stories that exist; we are writing our own story, being our own authors and co-authors for the rest of the world.
Gabrielle Harding

The first collaborators and financial backers of the Skip Garden were Argent (the developer) and the Guardian and the Observer (who had recently moved into Kings Cross). These relationships have been crucial to our success and, once imagination was caught, goodwill has followed.

Global Generation turned up with a drawing of a garden in a skip and I laughed – I thought it was funny and brilliant and that we have to do this. So it took about a minute for me to be persuaded. What I loved is that it's like a dream thing but then they were actually serious about making it happen. That combination of dreaming something, but being very practical in making it happen, was extremely powerful.
Tim Brooks CEO Guardian News and Media, 2009

Fortunately the work of raising money is now a shared endeavour. Over the last six months, supported by lawyers from Herbert Smith LLP, the Generators have been planning and raising money for their own enterprises. As Silvia describes:

Through the winter in cold afternoons in Liverpool Street, in an immaculate building with security passes, lifts, conference rooms, lawyers and buffets, the Generators became little entrepreneurs; step by step, they worked towards a Dragons' Den competition. Eight months later, in a room with cameras and microphones, three dragons gave their decision: "Pictures on Tracks", Lillienne's idea, received the necessary investment to be put into practice. The others kept going and elegantly prepared with presentation ready, they nervously waited for their turn to be called. Victory again: £2,000 was awarded for Toyosi's idea of youth camps – not at Pertwood but in the Skip Garden.
Silvia Pedretti

I remember when Nicole told us about the opportunity. We all jumped at the chance to work with such a law firm. The prospect of it was so exciting. Very soon the programme was starting and I found myself on my way to the very first meeting. It's here in the Skip Garden that it all began. It set the pace for the months to come. I met my mentor, Liz. She is a planning lawyer at Herbert Smith. With her help I was able to grow my business idea: Urban Camping. Right back at the roots! It's going to be extraordinary to see my idea come to life, right in the heart of Kings Cross.
Tyosi Abedonojo

GG's work is now evolving with the interest and skills of the new occupants on the development site. In September 2011, Central St Martin's College of the Arts (CSM) opened, just a stone's throw from the Skip

Garden. This is furthering the potential for imaginative cross-disciplinary work; for example, construction and fashion.

"Can we get hold of the materials on the construction site for a Big Knot project?" asked Berni Yates, CSM's Widening Participation Director, "I want to make a Giant Knitting Nancy" (a knitting device usually on a cotton reel with nails this time on a cable drum with re-bar). Within hours the call went out for cast-aside lifting straps and debris netting, safety vests and pipe lagging. The now-familiar sense of anxiety turning to anticipation grew inside me: what would happen this time? Slowly word got around and the wheels of construction got moving. Thanks to General Foreman Chris James and the Bam Nuttall team, over the weeks that followed a chorus line of trucks, tractors and forklifts entered the Skip Garden gates depositing cable drums and pipes, one ton builder's bags and scaffold boards. I watched faces of bewilderment turn to smiles as the makers of roads and buildings became designers of fashion and furniture. Giant looms got bigger and bolder, pallets up-ended created sports nets and story chairs.

This was the weaving together of not just things but, most importantly, of people: Kings Cross people. I stood back struck by the chaos and cohesion of it all…the blend of stories and skills from textile and product designers, young construction apprentices, office workers and local young people. We don't know where it is going but there is a shared sense that the time is right for people, place and space; a new space in which the possible outweighs the impossible.

In this journey of growing a new Kings Cross culture, something simple but extraordinary emerges similar to what Baudrillard describes in "Le Système des Objets". It is the extraordinary capacity of giving a plurality of meanings, a new and dynamic life to things. Skips, portacabins, bread trays, scaffold boards, water pipes and electric cables become the sounding board of ideas, passions and values. I am motivated by things revealing more than they seem, especially in our world which proliferates the birth and death of countless objects.
Silvia Pedretti

The Big Knot has now become a mission to create a multi-disciplinary workshop space, a mix of sewing machines and saws. Portacabins have been donated to create a furniture factory for the old timbers of a building site, to be crafted by young people and perhaps the elderly (soon to move into the new housing blocks).

These small stories speak to a much bigger story that creates energy and meaning as it is told. The story we usually live with, as Helena Kettleborough describes in her chapter, "is that you go to school, you get a job, you work, and you buy stuff, you die." The trouble with this story is that it's not very satisfying. There's no oomph in it. It's not the whole story either. Awakening to the vastness of who we are and what we are a part of, is core to Global Generation's ethos.

On our last night during our recent trip to Pertwood, flooded by the Generators' freshness, I looked at the sky and I thought about what Immanuel Kant said in his Critique of Practical Reason 200 years ago. "Two things fill the soul with ever new increasing admiration and veneration, the starry sky above me and the moral law within me." I don't need to look for these two things as if they were outside my horizon. The first one is the place I have in the world and in nature. The second one starts from the inner part of myself and is reflected in my actions with others. With Global Generation, these two things became clear in front of me and they immediately connect with the consciousness of my existence.
Silvia Pedretti

There is a sense of freedom in recognising that the creative impulse to connect what we feel within ourselves, often in immediate and local contexts such as the Skip Garden or our camp at Pertwood, is the same force that lights up the stars at night. It has always been at work in our universe. Awakening to the 14 billion year process that we are a part of is a fertile place from which to grow a new and positive future.

However, for a long time I was tentative about introducing evolutionary themes into GG's work. This has now changed. My partner Rod Sugden (who is a primary school teacher) and I recently ran an eight-day summer school in the Skip Garden for twelve young people, including Gabrielle. On the first morning it was almost as if the universe whispered in my ear, "tell it from my point of view". Around the circle we all took a leap and dared to think big and be big. During the rest of the project, for children, teenagers and adults alike, imagining ourselves as the universe creating all that we are seemed the most natural thing to do.

In my journey of making the earth, my experience was that I had to have a vision… I had to lead in silence to make space for the creation of what was going to be Earth. The creativity and focus allowed bright, colourful explosions to take place. It was a perfect balance of inside and out, hot and cold, fast- and slow-moving rocks, dust and other small particles. Large amounts of water, that we now know as rain, hit the Earth allowing a new substance to be formed, soil. The rich natural texture that runs through the fingers, makes me happy, to know I am part of that creation. Our Earth, the Earth we share today. I was scared and excited for the journey and the final product. Every particle and

element had a part to play in the amazing creation that took place. Each grain that was present formed our Earth.
Gabrielle Harding

In exploring the awe and wonder of the evolutionary process we discovered that our deep-time history really is a story that includes everything and everyone. The Big Bang Summer School brought together the different skills of many of our Kings Cross collaborators: gardening, arts, construction, science and media. It was important that we respected the cultural heritage of our young participants and so we included recent scientific research that indicates that clay may have played a key role in the origin of life. One of our young Big Bang Ambassadors responded by telling us the story in the Quran of life coming forth from clay. As GG's Project Assistant describes, stepping up to Joanna Macy's challenge to take on the authority of who we really are as a 14 billion year process has brought a new kind of energy and understanding into the Skip Garden.

Something about the atmosphere at the Skip Garden seems different this week. There is a sense of inspiration in the air that is gradually infiltrating my heart. I watch around me, and see young students learning about the universe. The Big Bang project has arrived at Global Generation. It's true that talking about how the universe began can bring up contention and opposition, different people holding different beliefs. Bringing this discussion forward at earlier stages, more as an add-on to other projects at Global Generation, it felt quite tentative. But now it has grown feet. It has become a building block, a more solid platform for many features that we already involve people in at Global Generation, such as curiosity, collaboration and creativity. The young people have been showing this in bucket loads; they are engaged, lively and serious.
Manpreet Dhatt, July 2012

Note to Chapter 13

1   Turner-Vessalago, B. 2013. *Writing Without a Parachute: The Art of Freefall.* Bristol: Vala Publishing Cooperative

14
The Dignity of Difference
June Boyce-Tillman

Between
Between the God and the Goddess
And the mosque and the synagogue
The bullet holes in the tumbled statues
The grass blades on the landfill,
The shaman and the cleric
The hysteric and choleric
The slaying and the praying
And the coping and the hoping
In the fractured rapture
In the hole in the soul
At the crack
The lack
Might
Bite
The Contradiction of "both"
Meets
The Paradox of "and"
Rebirth.

I was brought up in the countryside and had loved the Anglican Church of my childhood with its processions and hymns and colourful robes. I had gone to Oxford where the robes were less colourful and the theology more questioning; and I lived in Notting Hill with the growing challenges presented by racial issues and unscrupulous landlords. When this journey started I was married and living in South London and organising the first neighbourhood festival. This is the story of the spiritual journey that bore fruit in the interfaith sharing conceived as part of this festival.

The neighbourhood festival

One day in 1986 everything was in place for a celebration of diversity in South London. The dancers were lined up to tap their way over the boards laid on the outdoor tennis court; the roads would be shut; and Ruposhi Bangla, the local Indian jeweller, would set up stalls of Indian bangles. The Scouts were all set to prepare the hotdogs; costumes were coming from the Commonwealth Institute and local people were carefully prepared to wear the elaborate headdresses and gauze wings from the Notting Hill carnival. The band was rehearsing its countermarches and the harpsichordist had arranged to transport his instrument to the church for his Baroque recital. The scones for the cream teas were ready for baking. These were the plans for the neighbourhood multicultural festival. But what could be done on the Sunday to celebrate the spiritual dimension of the area? We had many Christian places of worship, embryonic mosques were established in several houses and the representation of many other faiths was also growing.

And so my interfaith vision was born. Some Christians had encountered the essentially Hindu practices of Transcendental Meditation or yoga. But interfaith dialogue was largely limited to hearing what different traditions had to say about death, suffering or partnerships. The notion that a multi-faith group might celebrate together with all its differences – but also some similarities – was seldom considered. Most interfaith dialogue at that time was not between ordinary people but just the leaders – the Dalai Lama meeting the Archbishop of Canterbury in the highly ceremonial environment of Westminster Abbey. My vision was different – that people of different traditions living near one another could offer a spiritual dimension to a neighbourhood festival.

This had to be approached slowly and carefully, treading uneasily on an unknown landscape – being aware of sensitive images of crusading armies with crosses on their breast plates; remembering Jew-hunts around Easter in Christian Europe; and appreciating the deep divisions that are common to so many faiths. Some chose not to join. One Christian minister called me at best sub-Christian and at worst pagan. The Jewish Orthodox rabbi wished the planned celebration well but could not conscientiously be involved. Wary of my own confusing Christian heritage, at the start I tried to be all things to all people. It was the beginning of a long journey of giving dignity to difference.

My interfaith dialogue began at the school gate, with the mothers whom I met there each day, Muslims, Hindus, Sikhs and Christians of various denominations. Brian Pearce from the Interfaith Network helped me to reach out to faiths that were not present in the school.

I started my journey by visiting the various faiths. I attended local mosques, wrapping any scarf I could find around my head. I went to evening prayer at the synagogue where I was entranced by the service book with all its Jewish stories and felt very close to Jesus who was, after all, a Jew. The encounter with Sikhism was wonderful. They sent a car to take me to the *gurdwara* and lovingly showed me to a special place amongst the women in the richly-adorned space. I loved the singing in the worship and the wonderful *langar* meal that followed, shared out from large plastic buckets. Since that day I have always associated Sikhism with generosity and welcome.

The Hindu temple was filled with amazingly colourful statues; but here I faced the dilemma of the *prashad* – a sweet paste-like substance made by the women, offered on the altar and then shared with the congregation. Some of my Christian friends had warned me not to "eat food offered to idols" and I was unsure of my ground. In the end it seemed ungenerous to refuse and I enjoyed the gentle sweet taste.

The encounter with Zen meditation was the hardest for me: the experience of two hours of darkness facing a wall punctuated only with the clap sticks and singing bowl left me bewildered and confused. The Buddhist who introduced me was a convert from Christianity, and questioned my notions of the ever-changing images of God. "Why bother with a concept of God at all?" he said. My upbringing had given me spectacles that were theist, and this was my first meeting with a faith to which the concept of God was irrelevant. I could understand God being there or not there (as in atheism); what I could not handle was the unimportance of God. This taught me that while sharing was central to interfaith celebration, it could not include notions or acts of worship.

As well as visiting other faith groups I slowly and carefully gathered an ecumenical group of Christians. This involved finding a local church in each denomination that was interested. The closest Baptist church felt they could not conscientiously attend without attempting to convert the other faiths, but I found one further away that was willing to participate. The Quakers were enthusiastic and my own Anglican church was excited. The local Salvation Army was represented by the head of music in the local secondary school. In many groups involvement depended on the enthusiasm of one person who would engage others in their congregation. The loss of one of these key players often meant the loss of the connection with that particular faith or denomination.

Gradually a diverse and informal group gathered together and took responsibility for planning interfaith events. We decided that peace was an appropriate theme for our first attempt at a sharing since this was at the heart of our motivations for embarking on this journey. The sharing took place in the Anglican Church in which I was deeply involved and included children from the local primary school in which I taught. The Christian venue posed a dilemma. It was, of course, filled with Christian symbols. Remarkably, all the faiths involved were happy for it to take place in a church. At that time some traditions of Islam, in particular, were unhappy to enter a Christian place of worship. But we refocused the space. Stage blocks from the local school were placed between the pillars flanking the nave so that the church was, in fact, turned on its side, with the focus away from much of the Christian iconography. Piano, organ and guitar were used to accompany the sharing. Later in the story of the interfaith event there were many debates about using the organ, which was regarded by some as a Christian instrument (even though some synagogues use it). Each tradition is, to some extent, defined by the musical instruments it uses. In the end we chose to sing.

We planned the event with separate sections for each faith, sharing little except some songs familiar to the school children, like *When I needed a neighbour* and the Jewish round *Shalom* (which has remained in every sharing). All these shared songs were carefully discussed in the group; but I was aware that they were all from Western traditions. The Christian contribution included a Bible reading and a wonderful tambourine dance from the Salvation Army; the Quakers read the peace declaration. The Jews chose to bring with them one of their very precious scrolls which was ceremoniously and movingly opened – a risky and generous act. The Hindus kindled the sacred fire – the *arti* – with ceremonial purifying of the space before the event and covering it with clean cloths. The Sikhs sang a hymn about unity between the faiths accompanied by harmonium and tabla. The Buddhist offered something of Zen meditation. The Muslims offered girls singing a song about being a light in the world and the boys explained the call to prayer. The sectional layout meant that the event took some time; but it held people's attention because much of it was colourful and involved movement and singing. We were in the foothills of sharing our faiths, getting to know one another, approaching each other with care, unsure of our differences and similarities, anxious not to offend or presume on people's generosity. We trod gently, aware of how close we were to people's hearts and core identities. It was a first encounter; and for many present what was offered was strange and exotic.

The development of the interfaith sharing

Over the years the interfaith planning group developed further. It had the single purpose of creating one act of sharing a year – although for its members a great deal about the nature of the various traditions was learned along the way. The secular festival did not continue and was only revived much later; but the interfaith act of sharing lived on. Members of the planning group came and went for a variety of reasons. Sometimes it was age and illness. Sometimes people moved away and we were unable to find a person with the keenness to be involved. We lost the connection with Hinduism and have for some time been unable to reconstruct that linkage. We lost the relationship with the Zen Buddhist tradition and made a new one with the Soka Gakkai International Buddhist group.

Sometimes people left because of disapproval of the way the group was growing. For example, I was interested in the pagan traditions and had developed friendships within them. One member of the group had a Druid friend and we expanded to include this very old tradition that is very different from the so-called great faiths, with the centrality of the Earth to its spirituality and the notions of a variety of spirits alive in the environment. The interfaith networks in the UK at that time did not include these traditions but I had encountered the presence of Wicca in interfaith dialogue on a visit to Salem in the US and saw no good reason why they should not be included.

The Family Federation asked to join, which caused more dissent. Originally known as the Unification Church, they were sometimes called the "Moonies"; for some of the group they were a "cult" and not a religion. But the rules of the group were established: no proselytising in the group or in the act of sharing. My position was that if people were prepared to keep this rule anyone could join. People asked "Where was it going to end? Was it going to be the Jedi warriors next?" I replied that this was an open dialogue in a world where religious traditions were proliferating at a rapid speed partly because of the decline in the power of Christianity in Western cultures. I myself had in this period explored many of the New Age traditions for my research on music and healing. I had experienced the new syntheses that people described as "spiritual but not religious". I had listened to their critiques of the Christian church and saw the numbers of young people in other faith traditions holding firm, while those in many of the Christian traditions were declining.

Over the years we encountered challenges that needed careful exploration. From the Sikh *gurdwara* came young women doing harvest dances. Were these a religious or a cultural tradition? In some of the faith traditions the culture and the religion were inextricably entwined especially when there were influxes of groups of people into the UK. The places of worship were becoming important centres for the sharing of cultures of the lands they had left.

This led us to discuss issues of women's bodies and what they are allowed to do. Some traditions found dance in our interfaith act of sharing inappropriate. Some found the costumes they wore unacceptable. The congregation of the faith in which the dance had originated sometimes objected to being represented by young girls dancing. Sometimes the objections were between faiths. What one faith found acceptable, another one did not. It led to issues around how the faiths each saw the body in their spirituality. The area of women's spiritual authority followed quite quickly here. This was interesting as many of the group were women. It became clear that the women in the faiths did not always share the views of their male leaders. We came to no conclusions; but the issues were well aired. However, the group has not included dancing recently.

The interaction of faith and culture was a continual backdrop to our meetings. For example, food and cooking have always been an important part of the group's sharing – both at the end of the final event and also at the planning meetings. The food needs always to be vegetarian and without alcohol to be acceptable to the various traditions. The group often contains a majority of women, who bring food to share to the meetings. The discussion often starts with how to make chapattis, birthday cake or samosa and so on. It is an excellent common starting point for discussion and where a group of "ordinary" people including a number of women rather than religious leaders (who often have men in the majority) are able to get together more easily on a much more informal basis.

During these last years I decided to become a Christian priest, and debates about the place of women in the various traditions surfaced again. Some of my friends had thought I would become an interfaith minister; but the journey so far had taught me that I engaged most effectively in dialogue when I was clear about my own position within Christianity – I moved away from my initial position of trying to be all things to all people. I had by this time explored many of the faith traditions as a possibility for myself but I had found similar tropes running through them – the role of the sacred texts, the one and the many within the concepts of the Divine and the problem of women's authority. I became aware of how much my view of religion had been shaped by my upbringing. It seemed sensible to play out my own faith journey on the familiar field of the Anglican Christian tradition. I could only be a Christian with a generous attitude to other people's faith traditions.

It was the interfaith group that supported me most securely on my difficult journey into the priesthood. I had embraced an inclusive theology including inclusive language and the journey described already had produced an openness to a variety of truths that were not often reflected in the ordination training. I shared with the group the difficulty of wearing the male priest's robes given my generous female body: the vestments hang straight from the shoulders which in men are wider than the hips; the shirts are mostly made of polyester cotton, an unflattering fabric for a larger woman. I had always enjoyed bright colours and saw no reason to wear the men's traditional black shirt and suit. I would dress as best I could as a woman and not ape the men's garb. I would still carry on being a woman when I became ordained. It was the Sikh member who directed me to a friend, Paramjeet, who with her sewing machine in her back room helped me achieve this aim. She created my beautiful shirts out of soft flowing Indian fabrics in glowing colours. I needed to tell her how to make the collar so that it would take a clerical collar but she made them to fit my shape and taste.

Over the years the group has worked towards a greater integration within the act of sharing. While we started with separate contributions from each faith, we gradually worked out prayers and rituals that could be shared across faiths. Each of these took several meetings to develop and complete and a great deal of discussion and debate; we gained a great deal of understanding of other people's beliefs and sensitivities in this process. Where did the Buddhists stand on the use of a name for God? Could we use the word Allah for God? This is often associated with Islam; but it is simply the Arab word for God and used in Christian churches where Arabic is the main language. Nevertheless some were uncomfortable with it. "Surely we all share the notion that we are the children of a Father God?" said one pastor. "No we don't," said the pagan who had a much more polytheistic view of the world, while the feminists objected to a male descriptor of God. To accommodate the belief systems of a variety of faith traditions and to find an inclusive language within shared rituals was complex and required creativity. However, it led to the latest ritual – a greeting for those who want to communicate across the different faiths that at once declared our origin while at the same time honouring and acknowledging the faith of the other:

I am a human being with hope and desire for happiness and for me being a (Buddhist, Christian, Jew, Moslem, Hindu, Sikh…) helps.

We were better at creating more material expressions of shared values. This was largely due to the skills of Les, the Buddhist. It started with a sharing on the theme of ecology. Here a great net was set up – slung between two church pillars; during the sharing children made pictures of wind, rain, pollution and trees that were pinned onto it. At the same point bundles of ribbons were attached and each person present was given one to hold to show that all the cosmos is connected through the shared environment. When the ribbons were stretched out over the heads of the assembled company it looked incredible – like a giant maypole; as the closing Shalom was sung, tears poured down people's faces at the sheer beauty of the symbolism. That same sharing saw the construction of a seesaw with ecological themes trying to get the world into some sort of balance. For one sharing there was a polystyrene bridge of peace that people walked over and met members of other faiths.

These schemes and plans often involve a great deal of laughter and fun. For the Diamond Jubilee the group are using the image of the diamond as the basis for the event. This time Les had the idea of building a large diamond with Perspex panels that could be put in by each faith and then lit from the centre. Everyone laughed as Angie, his wife, described how their garden had already been invaded by the polystyrene bridge and the see-saw. "Exactly what size will the diamond frame be?" she asked. Everyone laughed again at the notion that it could be lit by disco lights from within. Just having come back from a pilgrimage to Lourdes, I said that I could have brought back many Virgin Mary statues with associated fairy lights and indeed could offer a coloured waterfall with a statue of Bernadette. It is these periods of laughter that bring us so powerfully together and give the meeting its welcoming atmosphere; the party atmosphere facilitates greater dialogue and sharing.

The group's discussions are always interesting, for what became clear early on was that the boundaries between faiths for more "ordinary" people are not as clear as they are for leaders, for they are always synthesising diverse traditions while retaining membership of one of them. In the group the meaning of the term "spiritual but not religious" was beginning to become clear. A non-pagan member lights candles in the forest at the solstice. It was the Sikh in the local interfaith group who taught the group about how colonialism caused him to develop a multiple religious self:

Well, as a child in India, by day I was a Roman Catholic learning to read by copying out the Bible; by night at home I was Sikh singing the songs of the Guru Granth Sahib.

My own intentions broadened over the twenty-six years. In the first act of sharing I wanted to explore what the great faiths had in common and to establish interfaith dialogue between ordinary people in the neighbourhood. What could they share and what could they not? Only later in my circuitous route did I conceive the idea of creating a more life-sustaining world through gathering people from different faiths to think and work towards peace. It became associated, particularly after 9/11, with notions of peace, justice, respect and honouring.

In my role as Professor of Applied Music at Winchester University I have created a larger interfaith event called Space for Peace that uses the Cathedral as a resonant meditative space able to contain and merge diversity, accepting it without obliterating it. I drew, for the first section of the event, on a musical form called a Quodlibet, in which each part of the choir has its own separate tune and yet they all fit together in a miraculous way. The Quodlibet form shows how diversity can fit together.

Space for Peace brings together local choral groups from a variety of sources – community choirs, school choirs from church and state schools, the university, the cathedral choristers and quiristers. There are Jews, Christians, Hindus, Sikhs, Muslims, secularists. Some are skilled musicians, while others are part of the community choir movement singing by ear. A Rabbi and Cantor chant the Hebrew Scriptures. The local Imam calls the faithful to prayer. Solo singers and a saxophonist wander around freely improvising on Hildegard chants. In the third section of the event the choirs move to different parts of the Cathedral, alternating between singing shared peace chants and music from their own tradition. Both congregation and performers move around the building as they choose, lighting candles, praying, being quiet, participating in creating the musical sound. People become very sensitive to their surroundings and to one another. Some of the soundscapes become very complex as several pieces are performed simultaneously; some are quite simple with only a few choirs singing simultaneously. The effect has always been beyond my imaginings: in one event children singing *I think to myself what a wonderful world* merged with plainchant, Jewish cantillation and Taizé chants and motets in a way that saw diversity held in a unity that was not a uniformity.

As I write, this event in Winchester cathedral has been running for four years. Some groups have dropped out and new ones appeared. One year a friend arrived unannounced with beautiful glass singing bowls to play. A group of local Buddhists joined last year and drew many people into their chanting. Dance came in later and the contribution of the visual artists grows every year. Although the original structure was my idea, it is so flexible that it will contain new initiatives.

I am still on this journey; my vocation is to create artistic frames in which differences and similarities between faiths can be shared, expressed and experienced – where people are free to be different, but can yet share a place at an artistic table. I am working for a world where my six-year-old granddaughter can flourish. A world torn apart by endless "religious" wars will in the end implode in a way that might see the entire planet destroyed because of the intensity generated when faith is involved. My hope is that this work will contribute to a sustainable life for the planet in which all are valued in their infinite diversity.

15

Lost in Transition

Nathan Baranowski & Iva Carrdus

In the UK we consume our planet's natural resources at a rate that would require 4.5 Earths to maintain. We cannot continue this way if we, never mind our children's children, are to have a future on this beautiful planet. Transition Towns is a movement that responds to this challenge; an idea taken on enthusiastically by an extraordinary number of people within the mere six years since its inception. It is a movement that has spread around the world, with more than 1,033 Transition Groups globally.[1] Transition is at its heart about you and your community: your home town, city, village, street or house. It's about ordinary folk getting together to create and share local practical solutions to the challenges of our changing climate and the question of how we will live in our society when oil is unavailable or unaffordable. It's about knuckling down to the solutions (and enjoying it) rather than protesting or moaning about the problems, or expecting that someone else will sort them out.

This is a story about Transition Bath, from the eyes of two Transitioners – Nathan and Iva – as they become lost in Transition: moved, inspired and empowered by the achievements and possibilities, but also confused and challenged by the complexities of working with voluntary projects taking on a huge and pressing task.

When you experience the Transition notion of community sharing, learning and inspiration in full blossom it seems extraordinary; a different way of living in society. The task of living sustainably requires changes to perhaps every aspect of our lives: how we eat, shop, wash, travel, work and, therefore, think. People in a Transition initiative are striving to meet these challenges themselves, whilst working with others to effect a bigger transformation in their community. Transition Bath is a group of people working, voluntarily, to inspire their whole city to change.

So how do we get an entire city involved? Let's start in a quiet suburb in a typical Georgian home, though this day it's full of curious strangers. "It's just a way of being public spirited," comments an older lady modestly as she smiled quietly at the camera. Her husband is itching to get a word in:

"And we're proud of our house and showing it to people!" he beams. This is day two of a remarkable weekend, when a dozen families across Bath opened their houses to whoever wanted to see them. It's called *Bath Homes Fit For The Future*; and all these proud home owners had refurbished their properties to make them super-energy-efficient. For the whole weekend you could tour around the city, see a 1980s semi-detached converted into a glamorous retro-look eco-paradise, view solar thermal water heating on a Grade II listed Georgian terrace (a trail-blazer in Bath), or marvel at the home automation system controlling everything from heat and ventilation to security in the palatial abode of an ex-builder designed like the set of a Bond film.

"We're worried about what's going to happen as oil runs out, and we want to help people make informed decisions," explained one host. The beautiful thing about this weekend was that it was the perfect coming together of home owners – who had thought through the issues, made both good choices and mistakes, done all the research and found good contractors, products or technologies – and interested visitors poking around and asking questions. Because the hosts weren't selling them anything the visitors could ask what they liked and trust the answers. It was genuinely moving to see community in action in this way; people were so inspired and grateful.

This project shows off the best of Transition Bath: it was all the great bits that community offers – welcoming locals sharing their passion and knowledge whole-heartedly – together with the respect, resources and practical help that came with working with Bath & North East Somerset Council and a long-established charity, Bath Preservation Trust, that made the project possible. Not to mention the incredible dedication and many hundreds of voluntary hours Transitioner Cathy put into making it happen.

With projects like this to talk about it would be easy to jump from one success story to another. When Nathan prepared a presentation for Transition Cardiff he was amazed as he realised what Transition Bath had created: the projects seemed big and impressive, and all achieved with volunteers:

- a Big Event attended by over 200 people diligently organised by Jenny, Christine, Gen and himself;
- a Community Support Agriculture project, now a cooperative producing local veg boxes, initiated by Hugh and built by Jamie and the people of Bathampton;
- a community-owned, renewable energy company with plans to provide 25% of Bath & North East Somerset's total renewable energy,

brought together by Peter, Andrew and Peter from a discussion in the Energy Group;

- guerrilla gardens across Bath supported by Lyn, Iva, Sue and the Green Vision Youth Movement;
- a community nuttery created with the National Trust and cared for by Virginia, Jim and the Food Group;
- a Transition Talks series run and managed by Iva and Ailsa;
- a local communities project looking at walking distances and local amenities run by Dick, Isobel and Peter;
- a green schools project headed by Paula and Phil;
- numerous responses to public consultations by Virginia, Hugh and Paul;
- and now the organisation turning its efforts to fundraising with its newly-awarded charitable status.

But to focus on the achievements would be supporting the Transition myth that it's all so simple – a local solution to global challenges – and glossing over the struggles and challenges of getting to these end results. It sometimes feels like a relentless uphill climb to keep things moving, with the frustration and disappointment that can come from working with volunteers, not to mention the challenges of confronting one's own barriers to change. None of which are easy or simple. Then there's the niggling doubt whether what we're doing is effective: do all these projects actually make a difference or are we simply meeting our own needs for doing good in society?

All of these pressures and pitfalls can easily result in burnout. Even when things are going well, people plough their all into making something happen and then feel they need a cruise to recover. As Cathy commented once, "I think in Transition we're in danger of exhausting ourselves with enthusiasm." When progress is slow and there are setbacks the feeling is even more comprehensive: a deep tiredness; an empty sensation of being drained of all positive energy; disappointment or hopelessness. You wonder whether it has all been worth it. Like the last mile of a marathon, keeping going seems incredibly hard even though the end and cause is still relevant. This can lead to destructive anger and resentment of others perceived as not pulling their weight.

With "sustainability" the purpose of all we are working for, it seems ironic that sustaining our own energy is so problematic. The hardest part of burnout is recognising it is happening. It is so easy to overlook the key question of our own "inner sustainability": the ability to maintain our own positive attitude and energy for action. Inner sustainability comes from an inward-looking perspective more focussed in being than doing. It couples a personal resilience that encompasses the heart and soul and enables us to persist in the face of criticism. It gives us the humility to speak gently with someone who approaches a project with anger or derision. It is a perspective that enables us to inquire into our own understandings and prejudices of an issue that may be contributing to barriers, and, most importantly, know when to ask for help.

As Transition Bath celebrates its fifth anniversary it's curious that we're speaking of inner sustainability in an organisation focussed on practical action. Yet even after five years, for someone new to the group it can seem a bit of a mystery how anything works or how tasks get done. In truth, what it boils down to is this: do you join in when someone says, "I have an idea. Let's start a...", or do you become the person who stands up and says it?

If only someone told you that to start with, getting involved would be easier. Iva remembers when she plucked up the courage to turn up for her first meeting: a review of the year's activities in the local pub. She knew Transition was about local, practical, grass-roots changes, but had no idea how those tenets actually manifested into action. Who decides what happens? Do people ask you to do things? She remembers the awkwardness of entering the room on her own, feeling shy and not sure of how to find her place, and clutching home-made cheese straws – quickly feeling guilty they weren't gluten-free. If only someone could have been welcoming and explained how everything worked.

Nathan remembers how encountering the organisation for the first time challenged his ideas about how things happen or even why they happen. At his first steering meeting he didn't know much about Transition Bath or the people involved. Turning up full of professional confidence and energy to a dark and dingy meeting room in the basement of an office block, he met a roomful of mainly older people and mostly male. He felt as if he was sitting in a parish committee meeting scene from the Vicar of Dibley and he was unsure what it was all about. Though the image remains strong, reflecting on it the next day he was startled how quickly his preconceived ideas had skewed his perception of what he was seeing. Returning for the next meeting he realised this wasn't a committee existing for its own existence and policy-making needs, but was alive with amazing and inspiring people who had done and were doing remarkable work within Bath. Going for a drink with them after the meeting he felt privileged to be among them.

No doubt, despite our best efforts to avoid it, this experience is sometimes shared by others who encounter Transition Bath. Now, as Chair of Trustees, to Nathan there seems to be conflict between the formal procedures common in organisations and the necessarily informal methods of voluntary projects. "Where's your marketing plan and organisational chart?" one new member to the group asked at a meeting. "We don't have one and why do you think we need one?" Nathan responded. "You should have plans!" the member replied. Plans are great to have but are only implemented when the right person comes along with the energy, skills and time to fulfil them.

On the other hand, as a charity we are obliged to have trustees and formal structures of management. With trustees come an inevitable expectation of reports, risk registers and other regulatory items we can't avoid. Meeting these needs without the assistance of employees is arduous and can result in a few people spending their spare time on tasks very far from the hands-on community projects they had expected. "Can we have a report monthly on all our projects?" one trustee asked in a meeting. "That would be great," another responded, before realising, "Oh, but who would provide the information?"

It is really important to stay where the energy is, to build and support each individual's drive to make change. So when an opportunity arises and people have energy to seize it, we go with it – whether or not it's in any plan. Creating a community vegetable garden is an example. Bath is big on flowerbeds: after London it is the most visited city by tourists, and the municipal displays of perfectly ordered blooms are impressive, if occasionally rather bland. For a Transitioner they're also a bit too inedible. Our most visible project sought to correct this in a garden in Hedgemead Park, lovingly named "Vegmead". People turn up weekly to work on it, share tea and biscuits and harvest the produce. There's more than enough, so locals (often strangers) stop by to harvest some runner beans for dinner, and when curious wanderers in the park come over to see what you're doing you can usually ask them how much spinach they'd like. In a neat example of the circle of giving, Iva stopped into a local upmarket stone flooring company the summer it was created with a plea for slate to make signs. The guy on the desk squinted at her and said, "Didn't you give me some beans last week?" She had – coincidentally – and we got the slate.

Vegmead has also become a sort of covert outreach project. Iva headed over there one evening, passing a group of teenagers sharing a crate of Red Bull on the bench over-looking the garden. She hopped over the little willow fence to harvest. "Oi!" A yell from one of the lads. "Oi – Get Out!" He'd got up and come down the slope now – his name tattooed on his neck – and repeated his order."No!" Iva retorted, a bit confused. "It's MY project!!"

"What? You created this?"

"Well," she added, "me and lots of other people."

"Oh wow," he replied, "it's brilliant," and spontaneously hugged her. "I saw some kids running around on the paths in here the other day and I told them to get out! I don't want them damaging it."

Food-growing projects are a great tool for focussing Transition issues into something everyone understands: we all want food, we all want it affordable, and we all want it not covered in stuff that makes us ill. And most of us appreciate it when people voluntarily make shared spaces a bit nicer.

Becoming known for a project such as this one creates its own problems: people associate the charity with gardening, and unless you understand the logic behind transitioning to a city independent from oil – that it takes an all-out change in many different aspect of our lives and society – the fact that we also "do" home energy, or support Bath's local currency, seems odd. You could call it a branding problem.

It may seem trivial in the face of climate change but image is, unfortunately, important. We continually find how people's image of Transition Bath can be easily swayed by chance encounters with a single person. "Oh yes, Transition Bath," a lady responded at a launch event for a joint project, "I went to the Big Event and there was this guy who had such unrealistic ideas about energy – he thought it could all be created from our houses." On closer questioning she confessed that this person wasn't even a trustee, or one of the sub-group leaders – but simply an attendee like herself. And yet this had coloured her feeling about the whole movement. We've heard this kind of story several times, and though perhaps this works equally strongly in the positive direction (we hope so), it's hard to accept the conclusion that everyone involved is "carrying the flame" for the whole endeavour.

Transition Bath is seen as the environmental group in Bath & North East Somerset by many local people. To those looking in we are also often assumed to be a large organisation with paid employees. In truth we are still and likely to remain an organisation run and managed by volunteers. But expectations are high, both those we set ourselves and those of the public we wish to influence. We have all become accustomed to glossy banners and the all-round professionalism from charity stalls or public presentations. Is it realistic to expect this from an organisation entirely held together by volunteers? Or should we accept that this is what's required these days and do all we can to live up to these standards?

A tension between image, resources and expectations could be described as the "Quality versus Freedom" dilemma. For example, in a community group where events are planned continuously, advertising is produced by different people. Inevitably, what one thinks of as a good poster may be seen by another as too amateurish or as giving the wrong image of Transition. This prompts a management group to advise that all posters are to be done by this Poster Person, putting "quality" (of posters) above the freedom of the original poster-producers. Control has tightened its grip: we may get better posters next time, but people feel a bit aggrieved and some enthusiasm is lost by stifling the independence and pride in their own project. Leadership in voluntary groups has to be different from that of paid employment: if people don't feel respected, valued, mutually supported, they will opt-out as there is no salary to keep them on the task. And it is a continual challenge to find a way of leading that responds to individual enthusiasm while also meeting the needs of the whole organisation.

Most volunteers are supported by paid professionals who work for a charity. In Transition Bath we have volunteers managing volunteers, and it can start to look like a matchstick structure without any glue. It would be nice to think that there needn't be anything as stuffy as "management" involved here but the truth is that people come along with all different levels of knowledge and capability, many unsure of what they can contribute. "Would you like to help decide what we plant?" Iva asked the group of regular volunteers assembled at Vegmead one week. "No – just tell us what to do," they replied.

This fact that people get involved at different stages of their personal journeys toward a sustainable lifestyle brings more challenges. Communicating with a student who has come to the Farmers' Market for the first time is very different from talking to the chap who is using the old solar panel he bought twenty years ago to sun-dry his home-grown tomatoes. As an organisation should we focus on engaging people new to these ideas, with "soft" projects that emphasise the social and beautifying aspects of sustainability? This will irritate the hardline eco-warriors who will think we're wasting our time, whilst focussing on the initiatives they think worthy of effort would make newbies feel intimidated. We currently try to solve this conundrum with a little of everything.

Sustaining momentum is tricky when people's energy naturally comes and goes. A peak of effort is followed by a lull as those driving the initiative rest, whilst the people who've just come onboard are eagerly awaiting the next thing they can put their enthusiasms into. The Big Event – an action-packed sell-out day of talks, workshops and dancing – did just this. The energy and effort going into it was immense with last-minute planning going on to the eleventh hour by Christine, Gen, Jenny and Nathan. When everyone turned up the night before to set up the rooms, the workshop spaces and event became alive. There was a real buzz in the air and on the day it felt like there was a new energy around.

Our pledge wall quickly morphed from a blank canvas to a colourful array of pledges of action from individuals to take forward their own personal transitions; from "not flying in 2010", "insulate my home", "use grey water" and "get a water butt" to "getting the Corsham Energy Saving project off the ground", "writing a letter to my friend who is a climate change denier", "get involved in Transition and make a difference". Everyone seemed so inspired to take forward what they had learnt and dedicated to do something with it. Yet the weeks and months after the event seemed to dwindle into quietness. So much effort placed into one event left no one else to pick up the next wave and keep the momentum moving. For those involved in the organisation we were still recovering for a good three months afterwards. For those who attended it seemed they were left with an appetite for more, but found there was none.

In 2010 we were lucky to receive a Big Lotto grant to run a series of talks and workshops – from sustainable business to zero-waste cities and revolutionary guerrilla gardening – half of which were tailored to the students at Bath's two universities. Sam, a third year creative-writing student, attended the first event and during the discussion session made a sceptical point: "Why would anyone want to do guerrilla gardening?" A few months later he was leading a community vegetable growing project in his neighbourhood. This was new territory for him, and, being a student, reading books was an obvious source of information. After a few weeks we found Sam looking a little deflated: "I've just read The Moneyless Man[2] and I'm so depressed!" he confided, "I thought that being vegetarian would be enough."

At the most personal level Transition is a community of like-minded people. This is often what draws someone in. When, like Sam, you realise that being vegetarian, or recycling, isn't enough, and strive increasingly to live a low-impact life, it can be a lonely journey. Not everyone empathises with a lifestyle where everyday choices can make life more hard work, or time-consuming. So perhaps Transitioners cluster together for mutual support; you can talk about washing with soap nuts, not wanting to use aeroplanes or which uncertified organic local vegetable grower really is producing food without liberal application of poisons, without feeling weird.

Sometimes just the simple idea of avoiding consumption can be enough for people to start living differently. At the start of Nathan's involvement he was enthused with the idea of reducing waste and re-thinking his impact on the environment. He had a leak in his bathroom and so thought he needed to replace his whole suite. He recalls walking around bathroom showrooms looking at what he could have. In the end he didn't: he had a perfectly good bathroom suite and just needed the leak fixing. He had the lot taken out, the leaks repaired and Nathan and his partner scrubbed the old suite clean in the garden using eco-products. Often when people come round they comment on how great it all looks and ask if it's new. There is no doubt in his mind that if it was not for Transition he would have thrown the lot away and bought a new bathroom.

As we've described, being involved in a Transition initiative is a home-made rollercoaster with as many heart-warming highs as there are energy-sapping lows. While we may be frustrated by the hours spent in meetings, we enjoy enthusing people to make their homes more energy efficient, supporting local shops or cycling to work. But there is always the creeping anxiety that even all this is not enough. Whilst we can say we're moving towards more sustainable lifestyles, no-one can claim to have achieved that 100%. A sobering moment during one of our talks saw Mark Boyle (of *The Moneyless Man*) read us the riot act: "Do you think growing tomatoes in your back garden is going to save the world? It won't. Transition Towns needs to think bigger and more urgent." Like a bad taste that lingers in the mouth this is a reality we must use to question our actions on a daily basis.

Joanna Macy speaks of action from "the hands, head and heart". Transition groups lead with the hands – it's about taking positive action, and that's as it should be. But with all the problems that come with this action we can become "head" heavy – over-thought, over-meeting-ed. Without the balancing, rejuvenating effect of our hearts – the reminder to stay with our passions, with people and activities that bring us joy – we become wasted and tired with the effort of struggling against the current. Our prayer for Transition is to let us move forward with pace and a balance of hands, head and heart in all that we do, so that we stay connected to ourselves and others as well as the planet we live on. And always bring tea and cake.

Notes to Chapter 15

1   Much has been written about Transition Towns by its founders, Rob Hopkins and Naresh Giangrande, and we encourage you to check out their books and the Transition Towns Network website.

2   Boyle, M. 2010. *The Moneyless Man: A Year of Freeconomic Living.* London: One World Publications

16
Ghdamajori:
Migration, work and our horizons of care
Rupesh Shah

The piece of paper floated towards me across the small wooden table. When I picked it up and looked at the simple line-drawn cartoon, a whole book of mental maps was redrawn.

I often wonder whether Miriam Isoun – the woman who had sent this page my way – could have imagined the effect that her intervention would have upon me. I wonder whether she could have known that it would challenge me to think differently about my work in the world. Could she have known that in the fifteen or so years since that heavy, humid afternoon in the Niger Delta, the cartoon has been a constant companion, asking me regularly about the work that I do and for whom I am doing it?

Work. One of my earliest memories of work starts in the front cabin of a large red van.

I am sitting between my dad and older brother on the way to a gift shop run by our family. Perching on the rough brown carpet between driver and passenger seats in the compartment, I am enjoying the warmth coming through from the engine just below and from the two men either side. Dad is smiling and relaxed. He drives for an hour or so until we arrive at a concrete hinterland of loading bays and curving ramps, a semi-underground cavern, landscaped with large metal drums, precarious stalagmites of flattened cardboard, giant brown doors and strip lighting that suffocates the darkness. On arrival my brother, dad and another member of the family or shop staff set about hauling the boxes out of the back of the van to the back entrance of the shop, as I just try to keep out of the way as best I can. They work hard and fast; a flat scratch as the boxes are slid out along the metal floor of the van, a dull thwack as each box is stacked. The boxes are shifted into the dark stock-room in the shop and the empty van is ready for another load.

It was around the shop and my dad's endeavours to build a business as a migrant into the UK that I first began to see what work was about.

Our family arrived in the UK in the mid 1970s from Kenya. We were part of a Gujarati diaspora that had left India as farmers and traders, settled in East Africa for two generations and, when sensing the impulses of an emerging African nationalism, moved on again. Our family, along with many others, sought to secure some roots after touching down in the foreign land. We did so by setting up a stall in an underground market in London, selling pastel-coloured espadrilles, gauzy cheesecloth skirts and incense sticks that lent the whole pitch a musky aroma.

Along with his brothers, my dad drove the concern along. At first scaling up from the stall to a small gift shop in Watford, adding another in Wood Green, then another and then several more. Each time a shop became established they ensured that an uncle or other relative could be engaged to take charge. The kids of the family hung about at the chain of shops and we would be drawn into the work when old enough, joining parents or uncles during holidays and weekends – shifting, unpacking, stacking, storing, hanging together. This small retail business, called Situls, generated employment and work for a growing extended family. Many other families of the *Oshwal* community, who had followed the same migration route from a small cluster of villages in north-western India to East Africa, constructed similar family businesses here. Together they developed a rich financial soil in which our community here might grow, whilst writing the British myth of the hard-working Asian shopkeeping family.

My dad, like his peers around him and economic migrants the world over, worked hard. During the day he would be in one or other of the shops and then after closing time he would often travel around the country in the red van to redistribute stock from one store or family house to another. He would return home late at night, showing the full paradox of physical work to his wife and kids – exhausted from the effort, abuzz with energy of creation. He also put effort into establishing space for the community of Oshwals to develop in the UK, getting immersed in organising and supporting a variety of social and religious activities for the growing number of migrants and first-generation children. Though he seemed to revel in this busy improvisation, my mum sometimes seemed to find that the efforts that he put into the business, the wider family, and the Oshwal community were too much. She would whisper that all this *ghdamajori* – something like "a labour of donkeys" – was unnecessary. *Ghdamajori*.

And then he passed away – from exhaustion, overwork, the energy of creating or perhaps just too many good homemade *ladoos* and *burrfees*. Who knows? Mum's refrain took on a softer sound now, speaking not just of the results of his labour but also of the love, care and concern that went in to it, that had driven it along. Sometimes I even heard a hint of accepting, loving exasperation in her voice – like the sigh we make when observing a playful child who can't seem to see the boundaries that we have drawn but in whose willingness to explore we find inspiration.

Mum never played down the reasons for his efforts nor the resulting benefits to our family – both immediate and extended. I often heard others praise the work he had done for and in the community and talk about his willingness to connect. Like many children of our diaspora, I had been offered an economic platform upon which I should develop some more stability and security. I picked up a sense that because of all that hard work I could limit how much I gave of myself. So I looked away from family business, with its compromises and unrewarded sacrifices, and began to dream of paid employment and professional work.

At first I was slow in making the dream real. But I got accepted into university to pursue a degree in Business Administration (somewhat ironic given the entrepreneurial success my dad had achieved without much formal schooling). I kept my head down and aimed for a well-paid job in the City and achieved some success in this direction. During the degree I was employed on a series of short-term placements at the Bank of England. I began to fancy that my future would involve pacing the corridors of Threadneedle Street, rather than walking in the aisles of Situls Gift Shop.

And then I made a series of choices during my degree programme which had some quite unintended consequences. For my final work placement, I realised that I had an opportunity to "do something different" for six months before settling down to a working life in the City. With financial support and encouragement from my family, I found an opportunity to volunteer in a development initiative in a south Indian village. I was there to support local women to establish micro-enterprises so that they might better look out for their children. Immediately after this I spent six months of the final year of my degree at one of the world's largest business schools at the University of Texas; so grand that the campus had a trading floor where graduate students played around with real cash.

Upon returning from this year away from the UK, I contrasted my encounter with brash, uncaring bigness in Texas with the time I spent with a group of Tamil women who saw in business a way to change their lives. The difference opened up the fissure in the space where we hold questions about our work, about what our work in the world should be. And I began to wonder about the circle I had drawn for myself, asking myself "for whom and for what should I work?"

When back at university in the UK, I chanced upon the space and support to make sense of this. I opted to study a final-year module that explored the role of business in society from person-centred and ecological perspectives. The underlying (and unacknowledged) worldview of the degree had been affirming that the wider contexts of business could be treated as economic externalities. But through the module, I learnt to see that these ecological and social realities provided the significant framing within which any business practice made sense. These conditions needed to be taken on board by those at work as issues of practical, ethical, political, aesthetic and business concern and not simply marginalised.

I had become uncomfortable with the world of banking and business for which I had been preparing but could not see a viable alternative for me. An invite to continue studying through a PhD in Marketing in the School of Management seemed to offer an escape from that world. Benefiting again from the financial support of my family, I took up the offer without knowing where it would lead.

For a year I attempted to conduct my research into business relationships within the framework of business-as-usual that was held by my supervisor. But informed by an alternative narrative and supported by conversations with other members of faculty, I pursued a line of inquiry that sought to understand the differing paradigms of business, economics and human development that informed our lives. I began to consider the limits to growth,[1] and was troubled by what happens when corporations rule the world.[2] I began to think about the implications of a more life-sustaining worldview upon notions of good business and good work.

It was during these intellectual explorations that Miriam Isoun had floated the paper with the cartoon sketch across the table towards me in a humid office in Port Harcourt.

In the 1960s, Miriam had been a contemporary of the environmental activist and writer Ken Saro Wiwa at college. Together they had been involved in the struggle for environmental and social justice in the oil-rich, culturally-diverse lands, which had eventually seen Saro Wiwa killed. I was in Port Harcourt (a kind of Dallas of the Niger Delta) to understand the relationships between local communities, oil companies and non-government organisations (NGOs). I heard the companies claim social and environmental responsibility, whilst the NGOs were witnessing the claims of local communities to be suffering the consequences of the oil operations without gaining sufficient benefits.

The cartoon showed a group of six or seven people lined up in a row. At the head of this queue, on the left, was a woman bent double and hoeing the earth with a pathetic piece of equipment. Behind her stood an impatient husband monitoring her labour. And behind him a succession of serious-looking professionals, each taking their turn to engage with the situation in front of them: an agronomist studying the farming situation of husband and wife, a sociologist studying the interaction between the three, an anthropologist, a political scientist and so on. Each professional was shown with a notebook and pen in hand, examining the scene in front of them, appearing to notice only that which their profession called to their attention. A caption exclaimed, "so much has been done in the name of the Niger Delta, how much has been done for the Niger Delta."

Glancing between my interview protocol and the image, I recognised myself in that line of insouciant and blinkered observers. I laid down the pen that I had been using to collect quotes, stories and tales – the raw materials of qualitative research – and I sustained a foreshortened conversation, before scurrying back to my guest-house on the edge of town. I spent the remainder of the research trip in fog of questions, uncertainties and confusion.

Until that time I think I had appreciated the social and ecological issues facing communities such as those of the Niger Delta as intellectual issues. Though I was thinking about questions of power and legitimacy, I had somehow managed to leave my questions on the pages of the research papers that I was reading. Miriam's intervention motivated me to get beyond observing and thinking about the situation and find a way to become more engaged with the heat of the situation. My response was to scramble up my methodology, seeking an approach that would enable me to move beyond the position of distanced outsider and that would require me to account for my role in the situation. I was not sure of the implications of this emerging systemic understanding of research but it felt right. Having never sensed a political-self, I also tentatively sought out connections with other professionals and academics who questioned the relationships between knowledge, control and legitimacy.

And yet, at a deeper level, the cartoon continued to haunt me.

After dad had passed away, mum had stepped up and got more involved in running the business. She took on some of the responsibilities and eventually, with considerable support from my sister and brother, moved on to run one of the shops herself to look after us. Later my brother returned from university and decided to work at the shop. They had stepped up to doing the *ghdhamajori*, seeking to secure a future for our family in the mould of my father and others of his generation. I was conscious of being partially supported in my studies by their work in the shop, aware of their sacrifice and the work of my dad. Whilst not as outstanding as my previous prospects, I had reasoned that in becoming an academic I could still make a contribution to this effort; the financial prospects were reasonable and there were still good chances of secure professional employment. So whilst I was challenging the paradigm from an intellectual standpoint, the move to doing a PhD had also enabled me to retain a sense of my identity as an aspiring professional.

However, I was developing a growing understanding of the structural and systemic aspects of the current problems. I was also troubled by a dynamic of professional elites increasingly protecting themselves from the turmoil in islands of prosperity, shored up by their intellectual, expert and positional power. Another world would not be possible unless such attempts at separation were dissolved. Miriam's intervention with the cartoon was teaching me that I needed to do more than just talk about and engage with the problems as a professional. These views that I was developing about the future of society, social change and my work in the world seemed to insist that the aspirations, from which my increasingly comfortable circumstances were built, were flawed or inappropriate. The ideas also seemed to go against the norms of success that I felt were espoused by much of the Oshwal community. I didn't want to separate myself from that ethos of hard work and striving for one's family and community. Indeed, I couldn't make such a separation since the circumstances of my life were so much enhanced by this *ghdamajori*. But I could no longer fully accept that this worldview would be viable for the future we seemed to be creating. I grew alienated from the dominant view of work in community and at the same time I was equally disturbed by my own lack of grace in rejecting the struggles in which my life opportunities were grounded.

To resolve the paradox I avoided it...

Despite migrations across two continents over 80 years, the vast majority of our community and all our close family that lived here in the UK were based in and around London. I was living 100 miles away from this new homeland and so I managed the growing dissonance between identities by staying away and visiting family twice a month. I hid from view amongst fellow Oshwals my learning about the mess facing us all, the fears I held about what might happen, the challenges to identity and the possibilities of the Great Turning.

And at the same time I continued to invest more energy with this transition through the mode of a professional at work, earning a good living. As a researcher, I critiqued research communities who seemed to concern themselves merely with putting out research papers and making conference trips rather than engaging people affected by their research. But the only thing that I was doing was putting out articles and preparing my thesis. At some deeper level, I knew that this was not enough and was haunted by growing contradictions between my behaviour, values and knowledge. But despite challenging the attitude of separation, I still stood in that line of cool professionals, watching and talking about all the bits of the world gone wrong and far from that Nigerian woman bent over the land with her hoe. By avoiding more active participation as an engaged citizen I was able to retain some sense of legitimate but peripheral membership of the aspiring group of achievers, the conservative sons and daughters of migrants around with whom I grew up.

Then on a warm Saturday morning in early summer I stumbled into a green and pleasant world that shifted things dramatically and helped me make sense of the cartoon. I was responding to an advert inviting volunteers to help out at a community garden. Walking into the garden on the edge of town, I found air that hummed with insects attending to a vivid pallet of plants, flowers and bushes. I was guided around a hotchpotch of partial enclosures, a shaded forest garden with tall grasses whose centrepiece was a stout mulberry, a boundary fence woven out of ash and hawthorn filtering the noise from the adjoining main road, a brackish pond guarded by sculpted willow, a neat flower and herb garden cordoned off by rows of well-trained pear and apple trees, several growing plots alternating precocious vegetables with freshly-raked squares of dark soil waiting for someone to cast seed. I was invited to sit down for a cup of tea and chatted with some of the varied collective of growers. I soon found myself wielding a fork by its sweat-worn wooden handle and got stuck in with some weeding with a bunch of people from another world.

And in so doing I began to untie some of the bonds of the paradox I was in.

I spent about five years helping out at the Bath Organic Allotment, visiting at least once a week, getting involved in harvest days, drinking tea in the sun and rain, exploring new areas of growing and helping out with coordinating the adventure. I developed a joyful attachment to the community of people in the garden that I had chanced into. I revelled in turning over both compost and stories there and was enchanted by what emerged as a result. And in so doing I found that I could learn a great deal by spending time with others who had quite different histories of work and vastly different economic aspirations.

This has been the beginning of a journey in which I have begun to engage with the Great Turning as a more fully-embodied participant, with heart, hands and mind. I have discovered how to know myself as an active learner in this transition. And as an unexpected result I have become emboldened to talk more openly in the Oshwal community about my unfolding sense of the wider work I am involved with. When asked about what I do by members of the Oshwal community, I used to experience a moment of confusion and doubt and would proceed to offer the simple story of myself as professional researcher and academic. I would avoid mention of the arc of the Great Turning which had both reframed and complicated this simple narrative.

But the time spent in the garden and in other embodied encounters has liberated me to talk about a whole range of my life experiences and choices as an active participant in this transformational work. It has also given colour to the somewhat po-faced seriousness with which I used to see my work, adding a fluttering ribbon of playfulness and appreciation. And I have developed ease with a sense of self that is not defined solely by my trajectory as a migrant from an Indian village and an African city seeking personal, familial and economic security through professional work. I am more comfortable in thinking and talking about what I do in the world in terms of the earth, communities, love and our dance towards an unknown future.

Ghdamajori.

So heavy at the beginning, so light in the end.

The story of my dad's *ghdamajori* and that of many migrations is in some sense about the need to weave work together with both family and community into a comfortable nest. The examples of my mum, brother and sister showed me that work should be a way of securing safety for the group of people who will in turn support you. I had accepted a prevailing view of peers in the Oshwal community, echoed by other aspiring professionals from various worlds at school, university and work, that the main aim of work was to build your personal security through financial success and professional status. This is the migrant's story of escape, holding aspirations of renewal amidst unfathomed uncertainty.

But this story can draw too solid a line around the circle of concern. Our fears about the future can limit us when it comes to deciding which nest should be the whole to which we attend. Quite legitimately, we hunker down and concentrate our efforts upon those members of family and community that we know and experience as "us". Beyond this are turbulent seas of otherness – not to be ignored but not to be entertained or loved either.

For me the challenge of the Great Turning, like the journey of the migrant, calls for a focused, hard-working ethic of care and concern for others. In my reflections on the efforts of my parents and siblings, in my time at the shops as a child and in the efforts of digging in together at the community garden, I have learnt that this work ethic comes alive through direct contact, through living and labouring alongside. In that embodied contact with "the other" we learn to encounter them as whole and are therefore endowed with the capacity to bring love into being through our relationships with them.

The migrant, in her struggles for rebirth, knows this work for the other. The migrant also knows that it is the wider conditions in the world around her that forced a move into uncertain futures with a sense of hope that the work will be worth it. The Great Turning needs this spirit of adventure and sense of aspiration with a deeply uncertain future, but the work cannot remain inside an armada of tightly-sealed and isolated boats. Sometimes our history means that the circles of love which we throw out into the world can remain too solid, impermeable, fixed. But I have seen that they can be expanded.

When we make the migration to a life-sustaining society, it will be because we have managed to widen continually our horizons of care. The transition will have been informed by seriously playful encounters with countless known and unknown others, who we loved into being. It will have been informed by dreams of a never-ending pantheon of wholes – wives, sisters and cousins, living beings and universes, enterprises, soils and communities. Wholes for whom our *ghdamajori* have found a home.

Notes to Chapter 16

1   Meadows, D, Meadows, DL, Jørgen Randers, William W Behrens III, 1972. *The Limits to Growth*, New York: Signet

2   Korten, D. C, 1995. *When Corporations Rule the World*. London: Earthscan

Drawing Out Some Threads
Peter Reason & Melanie Newman

Our challenge is how to write about the writing in a manner that honours the provocation of our original invitation and the generous response of our contributors. Everyone has put so much life, love and honest reflection into each chapter that the process of putting the book together has itself been thought-provoking. In many ways compiling the book has become a living example of the guidelines described by Joanna Macy in her Foreword. In coming together to share our stories and give feedback to help deepen them, with all their underlying emotions and elucidating truths, we have linked arms to work towards a shared vision. We have witnessed genuine and often disarming bravery in the telling of the stories and in the willingness to ask difficult questions of one another and respond to feedback. Each one of the authors has been prepared in some way to face their fears not only in their chosen path but also in their writing. They have sought out ways to express the seemingly inexpressible, put aside the constraints of "what will people think of me?" and sometimes rewritten or rediscovered aspects of their own identity. Together they have held more than the shared vision of a book "written beautifully"; it is the vision of a light that might show a way through many other people's own inner and outer journeys toward a more life-sustaining world. It is this that has been most inspiring.

We weren't looking for heroes, only for people who have set about changing their everyday lives. But the experience of working with these "ordinary" people has made us think even more deeply about the roles to be played in the story of the Great Turning and the possible futures for human life on this Earth and in this universe.

The question, "Who am I to be, and what am I to do in the face of the challenges of our time?" runs through all the stories. Identity and the way in which we live, act and interact are central themes, interwoven with reflections on the unrest, uncertainty, disruption and discovery that questioning these very core and human concerns inevitably stirs in its wake. For some of our contributors, these questions have been with them since childhood; for others, they arose in response to new information or life circumstance. Responding to these questions often raises conflict about their sense of who they are: they move away from the comfortable habits of the "material girl", the "corporate lawyer", the "lingerie designer", the settled and contented life, as they search for a new vision and purpose and new practical commitments. With this changing sense of identity, people often find they no longer fit into old social niches; they disturb relationships with family, friends and employers and so have to reach out to form new associations.

Facing up to these internal and external challenges brings both grief and joy. We face the reality that the society in which we live is unsustainable, putting enormous strains on the Earth of which we are a part. At the same time, many people find reward, even happiness, in their new-found sense of purpose and commitment. All the contributors to this book have faced the threat of apathy, the fear and sense of hopelessness, that Joanna Macy writes about, and have done so in very different ways: there is clearly no one way to respond to the Great Turning. And in doing so they have all faced up to uncertainty: not just, "Will what I do be successful?" but also, "Will what I do make any difference in the greater scheme of things?"

In her Foreword, Joanna Macy identified five guidelines "to help us keep going as best we can, with simple faith in the goodness of life." What can we learn from these practical stories that will illuminate the guidelines? Each story is unique and complete in its own way. As living stories they will continue to grow, to evolve and to form new connections that we hope will be expanded and enriched by the relationship between the written word and the reader. To try to order them into categories would be to downplay their individual wholeness as well as their interconnectedness, both existing and emergent. So, in this final chapter, we simply want to draw out some threads to show how Joanna's five broad strategies work in practice.

Come from gratitude

While some contributors are more explicit than others in their appreciation of their immediate environment and of the glorious whole of the universe, it does seem none of them would be able to engage in the changes to their world, or tell their story, if they were not grounded in a sense of delight in and gratitude for being alive. So while Gil, Christine, and Celia tell of their simple reflections on the beauty of their surroundings, Helena and Emma invite us to delight in the whole universe of which we humans are part and within which we have evolved.

On our second writing workshop, when we discussed what we had learned from working together on our stories, many contributors spoke of their sense of privilege. Everyone had access to information about the state of the world; everyone could call on resources – not always money but skills, time, networks, neighbours, friends – to support them in the changes they wanted to make; and many pointed to formal and informal educational experiences that had both raised their awareness and provided appropriate skills. Others felt that they were part of a larger story, part of a lineage of thinkers and doers, which had enabled and given them courage; they felt humbled and honoured carrying forward the work others had started.

We were left with an impression that as the stories grew, so did that sense of gratitude. In many cases, what had started with an appreciation became a deeper sense of thankfulness: for people, landscape, perception, learning and other gifts, or simply for the inner strength to continue. For Rupesh, deep and continuing questioning about the meaning of work made him look with new eyes upon his own community background and appreciate the importance of spreading this ability to work for as well as with one another. June's inquisitiveness and delight in learning about other religions and cultures led her to explore her own spirituality and push the boundaries of the conventions inherent in her chosen faith. Annie's sense of connection with the life of the earth that lay under a piece of concrete started with a blackbird's song and grew to embrace her neighbours in a project that would turn a place of derelict garages into a source of joy for many. Elizabeth's intense love for the creatures and the life of the oceans prompted a restlessness that threatened to change her goals completely. This sense of gratitude seemed to be the origin of a compulsion to act and engage in all of our authors, which became manifest in as many different ways as we had contributors.

Don't be afraid of the dark
Clare's description of the Truth Mandala is one illustration of the importance of facing up to our pain. What struck us was the way that an intense experience of her own feelings created a wish to share the rituals she had found helpful with others who are struggling to come to terms with our world in crisis. We are seldom encouraged to admit such feelings as despair or uncertainty; they are to be hurried away from or surfaced over, along with anger, grief and fear. In her Foreword, Joanna writes of the strength we can gain by feeling pain for the world as testimony to our interconnectedness with it. If we avoid the dark, we also make it harder for inspiration to throw out its roots and for creativity to emerge. As a poet, Helen Moore is passionate about this creativity in speaking of pain as well as wonder. In the Web of Life Community Art Project, with its funeral for extinct species, it is not only the taboo of pain that she encounters

but that of death. These ceremonial and artistic activities bring home directly and vividly the damage that is being done to our living planet by our participation in the industrial growth society.

But another aspect of facing fear emerges in these chapters, which might be described as being willing to face the fear of the difficulties of responding to the challenge. Iva and Nathan write about the complexities and hard work involved in getting the inspirational ideas of Transition Towns to actually work in practice; Annie shows the challenge of facing the bureaucracy of a local authority to get things done. In facing up to the absence of employment opportunities congruent with his vision of the world and the difficulties of "authoring" his own life, Johannes finds ways to engage with others who experience the same issues. Celia's initial horror at the idea of giving up the comforts of a middle-class professional lifestyle to run a farm turns into acceptance that it is better to face the need for change now than be forced into it later when Peak Oil takes effect. After seven years of hard work, steep learning and frequent setbacks, she reflects that she would not want to return to their old life and expresses her love for their home and the way they now live. There is a danger here of making it sound easy: face the fear and everything will fall into place. In reality, we know that the inner and outer struggles, including the emotional ones, have to be faced again and again with increasing resilience and also with love. Each has their own way of approaching this, their own adjustments to make.

All these people are facing up to the absence of structures in our society adequate to respond to the challenges of our times, rising to the need to initiate and lead in the creation of new ones. The dark challenge facing us all concerns not just what we will do but who we are. And since we humans are essentially social creatures, "who we are" is bound up with our relationships with family, friends, work and community. Understandably, we hold tightly to our self-image and any move to change it may involve a profound self-confrontation that is part of the shift of consciousness that is so central to the work of the Great Turning.

Many of the chapters show how contributors have responded to this challenge, but two focus on this in particular. Patrick faces heartrending personal loss and the meaninglessness of the conventions that govern the life of a successful middle-class male professional. He goes "off script" and bravely explores new ways of living authentically as a man, slowing down, trusting his heart more. Kirsti starts at the opposite end of the spectrum with her childhood concerns about the state of the world and her early commitment to activism. But her identity as an activist is challenged by the demands of everyday life: first the professional role and then motherhood. Kirsti's important understanding is that there are many places from which to make a difference.

But make no mistake: these shifts in identity are hard won. They demand not only the ability to envision a different future but to adjust that vision in the light of "what is".

Dare to vision

All our contributors are driven by an imaginative vision of what might be. All of them also translate that vision into some kind of practical action. We find it interesting that these imaginative visions work at different levels. Some are immediate and practical. Gil and his partner Pip decide to install a micro hydroelectric scheme and straightaway get on with the practicalities and face the difficulties of doing so. The wider vision lurks quietly in the background: "Just one of many small gestures to make our tread upon the planet a little lighter." It is not surprising that Gil says that sometimes he thinks he has imagined it all. When he and Pip looked out onto the mountainside, they saw not only its potential for micro-generation but also the possibility of retaining its natural grace, even marking the line of the cable with daffodils. In contrast, June starts with a vision of multi-faith dialogue taking place between people of different traditions in the same community, and works toward this vision over many years. The Transition Towns movement offers a vision of grassroots work toward a sustainable society, and Nathan and Iva write about the more local visions and practical steps to make it happen in Bath.

We find that different qualities of vision exist alongside and interpenetrate each other. Jane and her colleagues imagine the educational potential of linking community and companies in the reconstruction of Kings Cross, using this as a vehicle for the immediate practicality of teaching young people to grow vegetables and experience the wider sense of living as part of a sacred universe. Annie's practical vision of bringing the community together and constructing a community garden to replace the derelict garages is coupled with a more spiritual vision of a life force under the concrete calling to be set free.

Sometimes aspects of the vision are in conflict, or the original inspiration needs to be widened. As an artist and a poet, Helen holds her vision of a funeral for extinct species strongly, and yet as she struggles to make it a reality she realises that she must also allow space for others to join and contribute. She cannot just recruit people to her vision, but needs to cherish their ideas and creativity alongside hers. And Celia has to find the love and courage to join with and build on her husband's original vision of moving to sustainable farming and a very different way of looking after their family.

It is also clear that we should not just seek big visions. In our meetings

Christine often expressed admiration for the scale of other contributors' projects, implicitly disparaging the changes she had made in her own life. We see what she undertook as brave and significant. She took on the compacting principles, not just as a short-term experiment, but over several years as a new way of being in the world which went to the root of not only her shopping habits but also her relationships with others and her sense of who she is in the world. She used the principles not as a set of rules, but as a way of learning about herself.

The principle "Don't be afraid of the dark" includes not being afraid of seeing what this does to you and who you are. It encourages us to look not only at who we are to ourselves but also who we are to and with others.

Link arms with others

Joanna tells us in her Foreword that the work of the Great Turning is a team endeavour, and this is certainly shown in the stories of our contributors. They also show the diversity and challenges in the process of reaching out to others.

June's work can be seen as based on the premise that if we don't link hands across difference – in her case religious difference – we are more likely to fight. She goes to great lengths to reach out to other traditions, trying to be all things to all people, and in the process may be in danger of losing her own roots. So when it comes to ordain as a priest, she realises it is important to base her work in the tradition in which she was brought up. Even with this return to familiar territory there comes a tension between conformity and diversity when she wishes to honour her femininity despite the rather masculine shape and fabric traditional to a priest's robes. June gives us a moving and memorable image when she writes of the Sikh friend who made her colourful shirts with clerical collars on her sewing machine. You don't need to lose yourself in order to link arms with others.

The Transition Towns movement is focussed on drawing people into local activism and might be seen as the paradigm example of linking hands. Yet as Nathan and Iva show, there are enormous dilemmas in creating and leading a city-wide participative process, in particular tensions between the freedom of individuals and small groups to pursue their own visions, and the desire for all activities to represent the organisation as a whole. There is both struggle and muddle in bringing the dream of grassroots activism to fruition.

Our contributors show that we link arms with others for several different reasons. Sometimes we need to work together, share tasks and skills, to get the job done. More than this, our contributors recognise that collaboration and solidarity are politically important values in their own right. But linking arms with others also brings a sense of belonging and the conviviality of working and playing alongside others that is of inestimable value.

Annie shows in her story of the development of a garden how different people brought their skills to make significant contributions at different points in the campaign. She also shows how drawing the community together was important in its own right and in order to build energy and support for the project. And through the highs and lows of the project those involved are sustained by the joy of simple association with each other, "...crowded around the kitchen table...poring over the designs, writing grants and drinking lots of wine!"

It is both the strength of the vision and the character of the protagonists that draws others into participation. When Gil and Pip said they wanted to install a hydro scheme in their property in Wales, they captured the imagination of everyone in the valley. Engineers, farmers, neighbours were all happy to pitch in and help where they could, often without being asked. When we asked Gil to write more about how they got so much help, he replied, "Neither of us has any real idea of why so many people helped us, they just did. I've always found people helpful if asked, sometimes without being asked, and we are blessed with wonderful farming neighbours." His reply is typically modest, not taking into account the way they themselves have contributed to friendly and reciprocal relations with their neighbours.

Rupesh's story also tells us a lot about linking arms and working with others. He shows how the Oshwal Jain community not only survived but prospered after arriving in the UK by working hard and working together. Rupesh struggles with the tensions between loyal membership of his community and making his way in the wider world. He realises that good work comes from direct, embodied contact, "a living and labouring alongside", and through this love comes into being. He also realises that the circle of love for the migrant can be limited, and that the Great Turning calls on us to continually widen our horizons of care. But we are all migrants into an uncertain future. We must be careful not to link arms only with those with similar views to our own.

Act your age

"We are as old as the universe," writes Joanna, and we have "an absolute right to step forward and act on Earth's behalf." Helena's story shows us one way to live this principle in depth and with enthusiasm. From the moment she first came across Thomas Berry and Brian Swimme's notion of the universe as a story of which she is a part, she has not just pursued a deeper understanding of this principle but has incorporated it into her everyday life as a mother, at work, and in her community. She campaigns to plant trees in her street, not just because trees are nice to have around, but because trees are connected to everything else. She works within her community, not just because community is important, but because by working together "we start to build ourselves back into the fabric of the universe." That this work bears fruit is shown by her daughter Nora, who writes how she and her sisters were brought up not just in a home but "in a cosmos of great age and size".

Jane, in a similar way, places the work of Global Generation within the framework of the universe story. Global Generation is about inspiring young people, linking the community with the construction project, growing vegetables in skips. And increasingly it is about doing this in the context of the wider evolutionary story of which we are all a part. "Awakening to the 14 billion year process that we are a part of is a fertile place from which to grow a new and positive future," writes Jane.

It would be easy to think that valuing our connection with the universe and feeling part of a living system so much older and infinite than our visible surroundings is only possible for ethereal types who live in the country or present TV documentaries. Yet here are two people who have been able to link the grandeur of these ideas with the minutiae of everyday life and dare to share them with everyone they meet. In fact this weaving of the majestic with the commonplace is another common thread in all the stories: a sense of our smallness yet our part in something great.

We have tried to show what we have learned about each of the five guidelines from the different contributions. But we can also see that the guidelines cannot be taken separately, that they interact. This is well shown in Emma's chapter. The story starts with Emma's excitement about her first job as lingerie designer in Hong Kong, one of the centres of the industrial growth society. She shows how, despite the excitement and the glamour, her work is meaningless and she feels alone and isolated. She experiences a profound challenge to her sense of identity. Her depression forces her into a dark place, yet she nevertheless finds the glimmer of a hope in the course at Schumacher College (Don't be afraid of the dark). She learns and internalises a new holistic appreciation of the world (Come from gratitude), but is set back again by the difficulty of finding a practical expression of this and of making her way in the world financially. Having confronted the dark already, she is now more able to respond creatively by founding Emiliana Underwear (Dare to vision), a business that incorporates her vision of sustainability that will also provide a modest income. But working on her own is lonely, so she reaches out to others by drawing other women into knicker-making workshops that are both convivial and confront patterns of consumerism (Link arms with others). But this is not enough, not sufficiently encompassing her bigger vision of the web of life on Earth and the mystery of the universe.

Annie concludes her chapter by reflecting that whatever may happen to the garden in the future does not diminish the value of the present moment. All these projects are significant in the lives of the contributors and tiny in relation to the challenge that we face. They are both immediately worthwhile and also contain hope for the future. Christine observed in one of our workshops that there is a seed in everyone that just needs the right conditions to grow. Perhaps, in offering a book of stories, we are scattering seeds. Some will fall by the wayside and some on the stony ground of apathy and scepticism. But others will take root, grow, and produce more story-seeds, spreading farther and wider than we can possibly imagine, reaching out to lifetimes far beyond our own.

Contributors

Elizabeth Claire Alberts
I work as a freelance writer with a particular interest in the environment. At present I am a scholarship-awarded PhD candidate at Macquarie University in Sydney, Australia, working on my thesis on verse novels and a creative writing project as well as teaching and lecturing in creative writing. My published work includes poetry, children's fiction, and non-fiction articles. When not writing, I volunteer for a number of environmental organisations.
elizabethcalberts@gmail.com

Patrick Andrews
My restless spirit and passion for life have led me on an eventful journey. For many years I worked as an international corporate lawyer and project manager, handling multi-million pound international deals for large companies. These days I teach, write and advise on how to build businesses based on trust. Living in the New Forest in southern England with my wife and son, I like to bake bread, grow vegetables and go surfing. My greatest influence is Gandhi, because of his relentless quest for truth.
patrickandr@gmail.com

Nathan Baranowski
Inspired by nature, I am a social entrepreneur and agent for change who is constantly seeking new ventures and projects that will build a more sustainable world. At a local level I am involved in Transition Bath, helping to build a positive and resilient future in the face of climate change and Peak Oil. Outside of change I love to be running or in the waters of Devon and Cornwall surfing.
nathan@transitionbath.org

Christine Bone

After twenty years living abroad on three different continents as a wife and mother to three sons, on my return to the UK I initially re-trained and worked as a young person's counsellor. I then discovered the MSc in Responsibility & Business Practice, a remarkable degree programme at the University of Bath. I was initially involved as the course administrator but later was able to join as a student. This degree changed the way I see the world and its impact continues. I currently work at the University of Bath.

C.Bone@bath.ac.uk

June Boyce-Tillman

I read music at Oxford University, taught in many schools in the London area and am now Professor of Applied Music at the University of Winchester where I run the Research Centre for the Arts as Well-being. I am a composer active in community music-making, exploring the possibilities of intercultural/interfaith sharing through composing/improvising and have published widely on issues of music, education and spirituality. My large-scale works for cathedrals such as Winchester and Southwark involve professional musicians and schoolchildren. I was awarded an MBE for my services to music and education.

june.boyce-tillman@winchester.ac.uk
www.impulse-music.co.uk/juneboyce-tillman

Iva Carrdus

My journey so far has taken me via a psychology degree to photography and equine-assisted therapy, through planting carrots halfway up a mountain in New Zealand and challenging children to get off the wrong side of their horse in America, to Bath where I presently live. My motivation, though it appears in different guises, is to help people engage with undiscovered aspects of themselves; whether through connecting with animals, plants or other people's stories.

iva@transitionbath.org

Gil Chambers

I was born in Walton on Thames but moved to live in Monmouth aged 12, when life began! I studied architecture and after time in offices set up my own design & build company. I always wanted to live in the countryside and build my own buildings, and I finally made it in 1993 when, with new partner Pip, we moved to Cae'r Hendre, a derelict group of farm buildings in the Brecon Beacons where I plan to stay. *gilpip@googlemail.com*

Annie Davy

As a woman, mother and step-grandmother, my life-long enquiry is human development potential: what is possible when we bring body, heart and mind into play with the substance of the Earth and when we work with and for all living beings. I have pursued these themes as a teacher, playworker, writer, facilitator and social entrepreneur. I am currently Director of The Nature Effect (*www.thenatureeffect. com*) and a trustee of Barracks Lane Community Garden (*www.barrackslanegarden.org.uk*). *anniedavy@aol.com*

Nora Kettleborough

I am a physics student at Imperial College London, though I will spend my third year studying at the Institut Polytechnique de Grenoble, France, where I hope to take full advantage of the proximity of the Alps. In my spare time I play field hockey, run sprint triathlons, am treasurer of Imperial College wind band and help out in my home community. I have always enjoyed writing and this is my first published written project. In the future I would like to contribute to making science more accessible.

Helena Kettleborough

I am committed to working with others to create a better world for humans and all the other animals, birds, insects, plants and trees with whom we share the planet, building on my skills and experience as a neighbourhood and community development manager. I am studying for a PhD in the Department of Management Learning and Leadership at Lancaster University, exploring learning as a way forward into the future. I am developing collaborative projects to share ideas about living in a planet and cosmos using stories and appreciative practice.

helena.kettleborough@btinternet.com

Emma Kidd

I started my career as a lingerie designer in Hong Kong. After five years of having experienced the damaging effects of mass-production and globalisation I decided to leave. I found Schumacher College in 2008, which is where I completed an MSc in Holistic Science. I now practice a holistic approach to lingerie design with my project, Emiliana Underwear – and I am starting a new project that delivers practical workshops for personal and organisational development which bring attention to our potential of developing a holistic way of seeing, being and doing. My main influences come from the work of Henri Bortoft, Craig Holdrege and Johann Wolfgang Von Goethe – all for their work towards developing and applying a dynamic, holistic way of seeing.

www.emilianaunderwear.wordpress.com
www.sensinglife.net

Joanna Macy

An eco-philosopher and a scholar of Buddhism, general systems theory, and deep ecology, I interweave my scholarship with five decades of activism in the movements for peace, justice and ecology. As the root teacher of the Work That Reconnects, I created a ground-breaking theoretical framework for personal and social change, as well as a powerful workshop methodology for its application. My work addresses psychological and spiritual issues of the nuclear age, the cultivation of ecological awareness, and the fruitful resonance between Buddhist thought and contemporary science.
www.joannamacy.net

Johannes Moeller

Born in Germany, I have spent most of my young adult life in the beautiful hills of Wales and Devon. I support young adults in building their capacity to catalyse positive change in their own lives and community within the context of increasing social and environmental challenges. I create and facilitate transformational learning experiences for people worldwide, including the Catalyst Course at Embercombe. Most recently I co-founded Edventure, Frome, a year-long education programme for changemakers.
www.johannesmoeller.com,www.catalystcourse.co.uk
www.edventurefrome.org

Helen Moore

I am an ecopoet, children's author and community artist based in Frome, Somerset. My poems and essays appear in a wide range of anthologies and journals, and my debut poetry collection, *Hedge Fund, And Other Living Margins*, was published by Shearsman Books in 2012. I regularly perform my poetry around the UK, and also work as a Forest Schools practitioner. Other books include the *Hope* stories about climate change for children (Lollypop Publishing, 2008 & 2009)
www.natures-words.co.uk

Melanie Newman

Early visions of life as an ecologist and writer suffered a setback when at school I was told, "There's no future in that!" Twenty-seven years later, after a somewhat single-minded career in business, I was introduced to deep ecology at Schumacher College. It led to a rethink. Almost all of my work now involves writing, taking a special interest in stories exploring our relationship with the natural world. I teach creative writing at the University of Winchester and I'm researching a PhD thesis entitled Real Life and Magic: an inquiry into the expression of deep ecology in children's fiction. *tomelnewman@googlemail.com*

Kirsti Norris

Aware of injustice and destruction to our planet at a young age, I have spent my life standing up for the environment and promoting positive change. Even as a committed environmentalist, I have found making some environmental lifestyle choices challenging. I am fascinated with how to promote and achieve sustainable behaviour with those that have less enthusiasm. I set up Action for Sustainability to facilitate the understanding of sustainability and empower change in organisations. *kirsti@actionforsustainability.com*

Clare Power

I am a mother, daughter, sister, friend, community activist, PhD student (researching the Transition movement in Australia), academic and child of our complex, diverse and awesomely beautiful universe. I live in the Blue Mountains, Australia where I love being with my children, having cups of tea with friends, walking in the bush, learning to see with permaculture lenses and imagining that humanity will soon embrace an ecological worldview. Many wise and wonderful people have been my teachers and inspiration including my family, friends, Joanna Macy, John Seed, Starhawk and our Earth. *bmpower@live.com*

Peter Reason

I retired in 2009 from the University of Bath where I contributed to the theory and practice of action research, and taught and led research in the field of sustainability. I believe the root of the problem is that too many humans see themselves as separate from, rather than part of, the community of life on Earth. Post-retirement I have focused on "nature writing for an ecology in crisis" in a blog and in my forthcoming book *The Call of the Running Tide*.
www.peterreason.eu

Jane Riddiford

Over the last 20 years I have brought my love of the outdoors, gained through growing up on a farm in New Zealand, to urban agricultural and arts projects which bring different parts of the community together. Thanks to evolutionaries such as Teilhard de Chardin, Brian Swimme and Andrew Cohen, I have been inspired by our 14 billion year history as a wellspring of creativity and purpose from which to grow a socially and environmentally-responsible future. These experiences are informing the Action Research-based doctorate in Organisational Change that I am pursuing at Ashridge Business School.
www.globalgeneration.org.uk

Rupesh Shah

As a lapsed academic, I forage work to sustain life. Berries in my basket just now include advising a community health-development organisation, tutoring on systems thinking for the Open University and researching the business of climate adaptation. Influences include Gregory and Mary Catherine Bateson and second-order cybernetics, Gergen's relational self, Freirian *conscientizacao* and the practice of *ahimsa*. Equally significant influences are three enterprising spirits, excessive anxiety over any form of waste, Sidrah Warburton, mum's home-grown ecological sensibility and a late night finish to a GCSE geography project.
rupesh99shah@gmail.com

Celia Sousek

Born and educated in Surrey, I left school after O-Levels and worked as a secretary before holding various administrative positions in the Universities of Oxford and London. Following my marriage and the birth of my two sons I combined homemaking with working in the market research agency my husband started in 1990. Since 2005 I have lived in North Cornwall. I enjoy reading, opera, visiting Cornish gardens and walking along the coastal path with my dog. In other words, I am an ordinary person having to deal with extraordinary circumstances.

cottage.farm@tiscali.co.uk

www.cottagefarmorganics.co.uk

About Vala

Vala is an adventure
in community supported publishing.

We are a cooperative
bringing books to the world that explore and celebrate
the human spirit with brave and authentic
ways of thinking and being.

Books that seek to help us find our own meanings
that may lead us in new and unexpected directions.

Vala's cooperative members
- suggest authors
- design
- write
- support the writing process
- get together for book-making evenings
- promote and sell Vala books through their own networks.

Members come together to celebrate and launch each
new publication. Together we decide what happens to any
profit that we make.

Vala exists to bring us all into fuller relationship with our
world, ourselves, and each other.

We hope you have enjoyed our book. We would welcome your comments
and reviews at:
www.valapublishers.coop/storiesofthegreatturning
or *www.facebook.com/storiesofthegreatturning*

 Vala